# The Missing Peace

# The Missing Peace

*Rewire Your Brain, Reduce Anxiety,
and Re-create Your Life*

Laura Rhodes-Levin

**ROWMAN & LITTLEFIELD**
Lanham • Boulder • New York • London

Published by Rowman & Littlefield
An imprint of The Rowman & Littlefield Publishing Group, Inc.
4501 Forbes Boulevard, Suite 200, Lanham, Maryland 20706
www.rowman.com

86-90 Paul Street, London EC2A 4NE

British Library Cataloguing in Publication Information Available

**Library of Congress Cataloging-in-Publication Data**

ISBN: 978-1-5381-8163-8 (cloth)
ISBN: 978-1-5381-8164-5 (electronic)

To my husband Ken Levin, my family and friends who are in this
book, you're the best! You have made me who I am
and I am forever grateful. Don't worry, I've left all the names out☺
You know who you are. Thank you to everyone at
The Missing Peace-Center for Anxiety for holding down the fort
at my clinic. A special thanks to Lisa Cheek, Stephanie Raffelock,
the rest of the Pinky sisters, and especially Rebecca Bloom
who helped me every step of the way.
And oh yes, as always, Thank-you Universe!

An extra note to my mother who presents as my antagonist
in much of this book. She was a victim of trauma.
She gave me many gifts along with the difficulties.
The most important gift she gave was the belief that
I could do anything I set my mind and heart to.
My hope is that I pass that on . . . to you.

~

# Contents

~

# Foreword

I am truly honored to comment on Dr. Laura Rhodes-Levin and her magnificent work. I first met Laura when I interviewed her on my personal development radio show called The Aware Show, and I was so excited to learn that someone put all of the pieces together for an integrated approach to mental-health-related issues. One of the attributes that is very important to me as a host is a person's story. Laura's personal story is very relatable as she vulnerably illustrates in her book. Her story is what led her to make it her mission to help people struggling with anxiety. When I discovered she came from a personal experience of anxiety and she knew there was a different approach that could help people heal, I leaned in to listen.

Laura Rhodes-Levin's personal approach has helped many teenagers, families, and adults with her well-rounded program and whole person environment, and her book is like a companion manual to The Missing Peace Center. Readers will be able to walk away with a useful set of tools to apply to tough situations and learn to self-regulate a balanced way of life. When I first learned of the spirit in which Laura created the holistic healing approach by appealing to the senses, using neuro-feedback, group therapy, and sound healing to address mental health, I thought this would be an amazing place for anyone dealing with any type of stress. Then I saw families coming together at the center to support their loved ones, and I witnessed the honest bonds that were created in this peaceful and connected environment, and I knew this groundbreaking approach was making a difference.

I love watching people fulfill their life's dharma, and I feel Laura is following her path to helping society reduce anxiety and provide a set of tools to live a peaceful life in this world. I believe by lifting one person, we all get lifted in the collective conscious. Laura's book and The Missing Peace center helps lift the tides of humanity.

With Gratitude,

Lisa Garr
Host, The Aware Show

# Introduction

I was born with paralyzing anxiety, forcing me to spend a great deal of my life steeped in fear. Social situations terrified me with worries about not being good enough and I constantly felt less than. I took everything personally as I struggled with insecurity, abandonment issues, and panic attacks. I moved from place to place trying to escape myself and I made many important life choices from a fear-based place. In my early adulthood smoking pot, drinking alcohol, and taking pills cloaked me in false confidence. That worked for a while but ultimately added an addiction problem to an anxiety disorder.

Today I am free of anxiety, and I love my life. I grew up in the entertainment field, but in my forties, I went back to school to become a therapist. In 2017 I founded the Missing Peace Center for Anxiety, a clinic that combines Eastern and Western methodologies in addressing anxiety, depression, and trauma in body, mind, and spirit. Anxiety no longer rules my life, and I can help others achieve the same freedom. Life, with all its pain, still happens, but how I navigate its difficulties works for me, and most of the time, I feel pretty damn good.

Writing this book allows me to expand my reach in helping those who are still suffering. To release myself from the grip of anxiety, I needed to understand why it was there and where it came from. I have discovered that it is in part *genetic*, and in part *learned*, and most importantly, that it can be unlearned. To communicate that I under-stand how anxiety feels on a visceral level, I share my personal history in stories, beginning with my grandmother and following me until the day I finished writing this book.

This book is broken into three parts: Re-Wiring Your Brain, Reduc-ing Your Anxiety, and Re-Creating Your Life. Each chapter is broken into three parts as well. The chapters start with my personal story, next the tool I have found to reduce my anxiety in such situations, and finally, exercises to assist you in harnessing your fears and make them work for you, rather than against you. Most comedy comes from pain, so I hope you have some laughs along the way. I share with you my lowest moments, my way out of tiny problems and big problems, and how I created my dream life.

May you, like my patients, find my methods successful and trans-formative and may you achieve the magnificent life you deserve to have. Welcome to the *The Missing Peace: Re-Wire Your Brain, Reduce Anxiety, and Re-Create Your Life*. I hope it helps.

# PART I

~

# RE-WIRE YOUR BRAIN

Part I of this book explores anxiety that is inherited through our DNA and how it transforms itself between generations, based on the cultural environment. It assists in the understanding of how our primitive roots as human beings still impact us in today's modern world, and it will begin to address how we learn to distinguish the messaging of our parents from the voice of our true selves.

# CHAPTER ONE

~

# Inherited Anxiety

## *The Trauma Baton*

My mother's trauma-filled DNA flows through my cells like a drainpipe clumped with panic. Will there ever be enough Drano to clear it out? Her mother received those fearful genes from my great-grandmother. This hallmark mutation is embedded in my family line. Does panic have to be a part of me? Forever?

Evidence shows that inherited emotional traits in children and grandchildren of Holocaust survivors get trauma that is passed down from generation to generation. I am 92 percent Eastern European Jew, 4 percent Eastern European, and 2 percent West Asian. I was not going to be a five-foot-six-inch blonde with legs that never quit and a stoic disposition. If my family had a store that sold coping mechanisms, hysteria and laughter would be our specialties.

When I was young, I slept at my grandmother's a lot. The smell of chicken soup and feet permeated her apartment. She wore a "housecoat," a mid-length nightgown with snaps down the front, and pantyhose with a light brown tint. At least one stocking always worked its way out of the garter, draping loosely around her ankles. But there was something very comforting about the whole thing, the soup, the stockings, the feet. It wasn't gross. It was just Grandma.

After dinner and TV came storytime. She regaled us with her childhood experiences. Our bedtime stories were more than Grimm. The same recollections, over and over. She sat in her big, gold, velour chair with my sister and me sitting at her feet on the scratchy green shag carpeting.

She spoke with a *thick* Yiddish accent. "I remember, Papa. He used to come in, in da morning and he vould say, 'Get up!'" When she yelled his words, her shriveled brown eyes widened, and she thrust her half-stockinged foot out sharply, reliving that along with this daily greeting came a swift kick. That was our great-grandfather, Beryl Fuhrman.

A family of eleven, Beryl and Rachel Fuhrman owned a small farm in Proskuriv, Ukraine, considered part of Russia at the time. They had nine children. Two boys and seven girls. My grandmother was number five. One of their daughters died as a baby, leaving a family of ten.

"Vee came frum Pros-kur-ev, its vas biggah den New Yawk." Her eyes looked up and to the left as she recounted the memories, shooting occasional bullets of spit in our general direction. "Dey killed my mothah. Da Cossacks. Da Bastards."

"Vee ver hiding. Me, my mothah, and Tillie." Tillie was one of my grandmother's sisters. "Vee vere in dah loft in da barn. It vas cold and vee had to sit quiet. It vas vet in dah hay. Da Cossack's ver coming. Three of dem. Dey had long coats. Vee could see dey had guns mit dem. She vanted me and Tillie should leave. I didn't vanna go."

"I said, 'mama, no!' She covered my mouth mit her hand. She didn't vant me to see she vas scared. I knew dis. She told me to take Tillie and run."

My grandmother imitated her mother, whispering, "Run, Clara. Run fehst."

She continued, "Vee should go to da voods. Vee ran. I hoid a gun go off. A bang. Dey killed her, my mothah. Dey shot her in da head. Because vee ver Jews."

And then there were nine.

"Later, Papa took us. All vat vas left. Vee vere going to America. To New Yawk. Vee had to hide in da snow, in da graveyard. Da Cossacks, da bastards, dey vould come through mit pitchforks and stehb into da snow to find us. It hit my leg; I couldn't say nothing. I had to keep qviet. Dey didn't get me." Then she would wink, indicating that she had outsmarted them, as she bunched up her slip, showing us the pitchfork scars on her leg. My grandmother never stopped feeling hunted.

Via Belgium, they came to America. Way before *Saturday Night Live*'s Coneheads, my grandmother hid her alien origins by claiming to be from Paris in her thick Yiddish accent. Because the Belgians spoke French, she thought she had been in France. Until the day she died, determined to conceal her heritage, when asked where she was from, her pat response was "Ve're from Frentz, Paris."

The end of storytime was accompanied by anxiety in the pit of my stomach because that meant bedtime. Even scary bedtime stories were less frightening than going to the dark room with twin beds, the kind that were joined together by a table in an L shape. She slept in the living room, even when we weren't there. My sister and I tried to fall asleep to the sounds of my grandmother's AM transistor radio penetrating the walls, at such a volume the Russians could hear it across the Pacific. My grandmother read the paper and listened to the news each night without fail. She had to keep track of potential hunters, robbers, and murderers. I lay there clutching the covers and listening, on the lookout for potential kidnappers, attackers, and killers of my own.

## Anxiety User Manual: Anxiety Is What's Right with You

Anxiety is not what's wrong with you. Anxiety is what's *right* with you. It is an essential survival mechanism. It is the fight/flight/freeze response in your amygdala, the emotion center of your brain. The amygdala, located in your limbic system, is designed to recognize danger and keep you alive. I want to help you understand your anxiety, teach you how to work with it, and embrace it rather than fear it.

When you understand what's happening to you, it is less scary. For example, if a woman didn't know what her period was but every twenty-eight days she bled profusely, cried, hated her life and all the people in it, she would think she was dying. But because she *understands* what is happening to her, that she is shedding an unfertilized egg and not dying, she accepts it as a normal part of life. She takes ibuprofen and everyone, hopefully, grins and bears it. Access to knowledge about our bodies and how they work can normalize otherwise frightening circumstances.

Let's take a moment to understand why your anxiety is part of your primal makeup. Imagine you are a child, playing in a meadow with your friends. You hear a rustle in the bushes, so you turn to see what's making the noise and see a big, fuzzy face. Then . . . it eats your friend! You just met a lion for the first time. That moment goes into your emotion center and stays there. Emotional recall that lions will eat you can keep you alive! This way, the next time you hear a rustle in the bushes and see the fuzzy face you will run. This is why your anxiety is essential. Be grateful for your anxiety—it means your brain is working.

That being said, the more "lions" you encounter in life, the more sensitive your emotion center becomes and the more easily your anxiety gets triggered. Your limbic system has now *learned* to be anxious. So much so that it becomes overreactive. I will explain more about *learned anxiety* in chapter 4.

The lion example briefly addresses learned anxiety and why anxiety is essential to our survival, but what about the anxiety you inherited? The high alert you've had your whole life. Have you ever thought, *I feel like I was born this way*. Perhaps you were. I was. I understand now why at four years old I was terrified of an imaginary bear in my closet. My need to be on the lookout was embedded in my DNA, just like my hair color. The genetic memory of my grandmother being hunted for many years in her life was passed down to my mother and then to me.

If you were born with brown hair like your parents or grandparents, you can bleach it blond. It will still grow back the color brown; the change is only temporary. You can put contact lenses in your eyes to change their color, but this does not change the true hue of your eyes.

Anxiety is different. We can alter your body's anxiety levels. The wiring in your limbic system can change. The emotional brain you inherited does not have to run your life forever. In this book, you will learn how to re-wire your alert system from both inherited and learned fears.

Please let me reiterate that anxiety is *not* what's wrong with you. It is what's *right* with you. However, if it has begun to limit your activities and rule your daily life, some tools can help you change it. You can learn to recognize the difference between real threats versus inherited or learned fears. Remember, when you understand what is happening to you, it is less scary. Sometimes it's not a lion. It may just be someone or something dressed up in a lion costume that *appears* to be dangerous but poses no true threat.

With practice and skill-building, your anxiety will kick in when there is *actual* danger but you will ignore unlikely threats. You will find yourself with a clear mind and the energy to create the life you want.

I don't always respond well when I'm given homework in a book I'm reading, so consider the tools at the end of each chapter a suggestion. If you choose not to do them, don't be hard on yourself. But, if you're up for it and you practice the skills I am presenting, you will find your inherited and learned anxiety begin to slip away.

## Build Your Toolkit

It is time to create an Anxiety User Manual journal for yourself. Think of it as drafting your owner's user manual, kind of like the one that comes with a car. You can buy a blank-paged journal, use a composition book, or find an unused spiral notebook. Whatever it is, make it exclusive to the tools you gather while reading this book. Then go over the next few questions and write out the answers.

1. Take some time and think back on your parents and grandparents.
2. Write down the kind of traumas they may have had.
3. Write how it does show in their emotional states and behavior.
4. Write about where these traits show up in you. For example, were they poor therefore causing you to have financial fears that don't align with your actual financial circumstances? Or did they experience brutality at the force of authority creating an odd disdain for police when they have no real cause to feel that way?
5. Write down the top ten things you fear most.
6. Are they real fears? Or are they inherited fears that have morphed to create unrealistic worries in your life that are not likely to happen?

By doing this repeatedly, both now in the exercise and in the face of future fear, you will learn how to recognize the difference between real and imagined threats.

# CHAPTER TWO

~

# Trauma Morphs

My mother and my aunt, my mother's sister, eight years her junior, were raised on a steady diet of borscht and paranoia. In my grandmother's efforts to protect them, she became the scariest part of their lives. The hunted became the hunter. The combination of a vicious mother superior and a Keystone Cop, she stalked her daughters in a vain effort to ensure their safety, driving them to hate and resent my grandmother until the day she died.

My mother escaped her abusive, early years by losing herself in film. She repeated her stories the same way my grandmother did, except my mother does not have a Yiddish accent. Her cadence is along the lines of a breathy Hollywood actress.

Her demeanor became glamorous, and she sucked in her cheeks to accentuate her bone structure. "I would lose myself in movies and act out the scenes in my bedroom."

Her voice deepened. "I watched Bette Davis in *All about Eve* and Olivia de Havilland in *Snake Pit*." Her arm stretched outward as if someone was about to kiss her hand. Then the charade ended, and the hatred crept into her furrowed brow, as her jaw clenched. You could see her uneven bottom teeth as her lips curled back.

"My mother was a crazy person!" she recalled with venom. "When I decided to run away from home at sixteen to live with my actor friends, she ripped my car keys from me and threw them down the trash shoot to stop me from going, so I called a taxi. She ran out after me waving a clothes hanger and told the taxi driver she would kill him if he drove off with me. I looked at him like my life depended on this ride. I guess I was so pathetic he felt bad for me."

"Get in," he said, and we screeched away from the curb.

My mother's hateful memories continued. "A month later she burst through my apartment front door, pushed past my roommates, and dragged me down the hall by my hair. Can you believe that?! By my hair!"

Record scratch. Of course, I could believe that. I had co-starred with my mother in "Fist Full of Follicles" many times. My mother's rage both inherited and learned was embedded in her coping mechanisms. In fairness back in the 1970s hitting your kids was par for the course.

Just like she had, I hated living at home. I wanted to run away and go live with my father. She wouldn't let me. I begged this request on many occasions and failed to bring it to fruition. My final attempt was thought out rather than blurted in the heat of the moment. I planned to tell her when we were having a good time, in hopes she would see it from my point of view.

Having spent the day shopping at Marshall's and "schmorking it up" with a delicious lunch at Mort's deli, she was in a good mood. I was nervous all day. Every time I mustered the courage, adrenaline and nausea filled my stomach, and I choked back the request. As we drove down Balboa Boulevard the moment seemed right.

"Mom, I've been thinking," I said.

"Okay," she said. "What about?"

Trying to make my case reasonable, "I'm fourteen years old, and I want to be able to experience my life fully. So, I was thinking . . . living in the Valley only gives me one perspective about life. I've gone to school with the same people my whole life."

She interrupts. "Where are you going with this?"

The tension in the car spiked quickly. *Just say it before it's too late.*

My dry mouth gulped down air. "I think it would help me be more well-rounded if I went to live with dad for a few months."

Her pleasant mood evaporated in a nanosecond and exploded. The car screeched to the side of the road. I can still feel my neck stiffening from the sudden jerk of the wheel. Before I could release my grip from the door, she had grabbed me by the hair. She began smacking me and punching me. Smacking I was used to but the punching thing only ever happened this once.

Her face twisted with hurt and she screamed, "You are the most ungrateful child! How could you do this to me?!" Bam, another smack.

"I could kill you right now! It's never enough! What about me?" She grabbed me by the shoulders and started to shake me. "You only think about yourself! I give you everything!" My hair was being yanked from both sides. "If you think you are moving to your father's you've got another thing coming, LADY!" Her voice was piercing.

"You are grounded! You're not going anywhere! Do you understand me?" Her eyes glared into mine. I could feel her breath on my face. I was in shock. I said nothing. I just stared back. Something made her stop and we drove home in silence.

## Anxiety User Manual: Always under Anger Is Fear

Today I understand my mother's anger. I know why my grandmother held anger. The frightening thought of having a daughter leave home led both my grandmother and my mother into a blind rage. One word explains it all: FEAR. *Always, 100 percent of the time, under anger is fear*. Remember anxiety is our fight/flight/freeze response. Some people can't move, some run, and some people fight. The catalyst for all three reactions is fear.

When closely examined flight and freeze are the more obvious signs of fear. If something runs away, fear is easy to infer. The freeze response is a little more subtle, but nevertheless, it does not appear confrontational. The deer in headlights look is not a threatening one. The fight response is different. It is an aggressive response to fear and may not be easily interpreted as such, but it is fear. When people are scared, they sometimes get angry. That's why people become irate when they are cut off on the freeway. Their lives felt threatened. There was a sense of danger. This is innate programming. When an animal gets alarmed, it gets puffed up and scary-looking, and if you get too close it will lash out.

News flash! We are animals. Animals with an ego-maniacal frontal cortex that believes it controls everything. Your emotion center is the primitive part of your brain. The frontal cortex, the thinking part of your brain, is in another location. When you are angry, the pathway that connects emotion and logic has been shut down. The emotion center is no longer engaged with the frontal cortex when we become highly emotional. Therefore, we can't think our way out of anger. This is like scratching your head to stop your foot from itching. It cannot be done. So, we must learn ways to calm ourselves to regain access to logic. Granted, this is no easy task owing to the biological predicament that the doorway to logic might be slammed shut. The higher your levels of hostility the harder it is to access the frontal cortex and logical thinking.

To help yourself, use phrases like "Count to ten before you react." And "Pause." These may seem like trite and overused sayings, but they are so often under-utilized and under-estimated. I think ten seconds is a bit short, but it's a good start to acquiring some time to calm yourself down until you can regain access to strategic thinking. Taking a long breath gives your brain a chance to escape from the desperate grip of your emotion center. Personally, I prefer at least a good twenty-four hours to process when I'm really angry or hurt. With practice the instinct to give yourself some space becomes second nature and creates the opportunity to break from a defensive standpoint. You will find many more tools to help you step back throughout the book.

When parents scream at their children in a misguided effort to express concern, the message is lost. Children do not receive anger as protection. They perceive it as assault. Anger frightens them and teaches them that vulnerability is unsafe. Even as adults, we do not feel protection or love when we are the recipients of anger unless we are adept with our emotional tools. We don't see the fear underneath the anger. We sense an attack.

Don't get me wrong, anger is important. The purpose of anger is often misused and misunderstood. Think of anger as being like a fever when you are sick. Fever signals to you there is an infection in your body. To stop the fever, you address the illness. The fever is present to help you recognize you are sick. It is an alert system.

Anger is an alert system, just like fever. Your hurts and your worries are the infection. Fear and pain are the real problems that must be addressed to return to your state of well-being. Anger can represent many things: danger, crossing of boundaries, feelings of invisibility, perception of worthlessness, not being heard, neglect, low self-esteem, abuse, and so on. It's your brain's way of asking you to stand up for yourself, to protect yourself. You are screaming inside and/or outside because you are afraid that your needs are not being met.

I've listed some examples from obvious to subtle to get you started on the journey of analyzing the fear underneath anger. Anger runs the gamut from frustration to fury. Let's examine anger from both directions. First, the anger we feel for someone or something else, and then anger that is directed at us from another person.

Incident: You feel physically threatened.
Fear: Safety for self or survival.
Incident: A close relation doesn't return your call.
Fear: Abandonment/not being liked or cared about.
Incident: Judgment by others.
Fear: Not being good enough or not feeling seen.
Incident: The family picks a restaurant you don't like.
Fear: My needs or opinions don't matter.
Incident: Not being paid enough.
Fear: Basic needs not being met or feeling undervalued.
Incident: The person at the cable company put you on hold again and this is your fifth call.
Fear: Powerlessness and unimportance; abandonment.

The list goes on and on, but *always* under anger is . . . yup, fear. The good news is once you understand what scares you, you're one step closer to executing the solution and getting your needs met. Not everyone can meet your needs, but you can. The person at the cable company might keep you on hold, but if you adjust your inner angst and frustration long enough to sit back and get your goal accomplished you will feel better, and your service will get fixed.

Now look at it from the other side. Someone is angry with *you*. You might feel attacked. Becoming defensive can be automatic. However, with deeper examination, you may see it differently. You will realize that the person who is being aggressive toward you has now lost their grip on logic. They are angry, meaning they are frightened. Knowing an animal is scared is a lot easier to deal with than an animal you perceive as mad. If a cat is arched and hissing, you need to examine the situation. First, remember the cat is scared. Then plan your strategy. Do you need to back away and avoid an attack, or do you need to help it feel safe before you approach?

> Incident: Your partner is screaming at you because you are late for dinner.
> Fear: Partner feels unimportant or underappreciated.
> Incident: Physical aggression toward you.
> Fear: Person is experiencing powerlessness, therefore going to extreme measures to dominate.
> Incident: A parent is furious that you missed your curfew.
> Fear: Parent is worried or feeling disrespected.
> Incident: Someone flips you off on the freeway.
> Fear: You cut them off and scared the bejesus out of them.

Please understand I am not attempting to justify a person's anger, I am trying to help you understand the anger so that you can interpret the experience for what it is at its core. Anger is a response to vulnerability born out of fear. Fear creates anxiety. If you realize there is vulnerability, anger directed at you becomes a problem you can potentially solve with the right tools.

We can't always resolve another person's anger but conceptualizing it on a deeper level makes it less scary, less personal, and more manageable. We can respond, then, with empathy, or with understanding. We can learn to walk away or to put distance between you and the angry person when it is necessary. If we learn to see to the roots of anger both, administered and received, we can better address the predicament and create harmony.

It may take you a while to trace your anger to fear. It may not seem like fear at all but trust me, it is. The more familiar you become with the fears propping up your anger, the easier it will be to recognize it in others. Wouldn't it be nice to get your needs met instead of being angry that they aren't being met? Taking an objective approach gives you a chance to determine the outcome you're striving for.

## Build Your Toolkit

Get out the user manual you started in the last chapter. Let's learn how to begin recognizing that when you are angry you are in a defensive state, like a porcupine with its quills raised high in the air.

1. Make three columns.
2. In the first column write the name of the person you were mad at the last time you got angry.
3. In the second column write what you were angry about.
4. Now dig deeper. Ask yourself, "What is the fear beneath the anger I had? What was I afraid of then? What need of mine was not being met?"
5. In the third column write the fear that was under the anger.
6. Repeat the process with the five top times you were angry in your life.
7. What is the solution or goal you'd like to achieve if you could handle this situation with clear thinking?
8. Write a paragraph imagining the desired results.

Perhaps the situation not only resolves itself, but it gets better!

~

# CHAPTER THREE

# Pleased-to-Meet-Your-Needs Invisible Children

My grandmother's trauma, intense rage, and underlying fear left my mother at the mercy of my grandmother's irrational and damaging behavior. She did not know how to nurture my mother. It did not even occur to her to do so. Her parenting didn't involve raising a child to become her best self. It was about survival. Keep yourself and your children alive at all costs. Keep a roof over your head, food on the table, and above all, steer clear of danger. That approach did not account for my mother's wants and desires. My mother's development was cloaked by the clouds of my grandmother's fear.

My mother's desperate and unsuccessful desire to feel visible and relevant damaged her psyche. When a person is neglected and abused, they often develop dysfunctional coping mechanisms, or in extreme cases, they develop personality disorders. In my mother's case, this manifested as a severe case of narcissistic personality disorder.

People who suffer from personality disorders do not often realize they do. Because it is born from a need to protect themselves, pointing it out is no easy task, even for a therapist. Personality disorders are thought to be untreatable, but I have seen cases that indicate otherwise. They can be hard to reverse or keep in remission, but with vigilant work and practice they too can be healed or reduced in severity.

In my mother's case, she has no idea whatsoever that this disorder exists in her, and she would be *extremely* hurt and, therefore angry, at anyone who might suggest it. She runs from one problem to another without stopping to look inward, hence her five marriages. You can't hit a moving target, so best to keep running.

My brother was born during her first marriage whereas my sister and I came from husband two, who raised all three of us. Our needs as her children were unseen, just as the needs she and her sister had were invisible to my grandmother.

The Super 8 film of my first birthday party shows me dwarfed by a gigantic living room chair. My pink party dress spread like a fan on the gold velvet, revealing my opaque white stockings. A taffeta bow perched on my head with the aid of Vaseline, and my eyebrows contorted in a desperate attempt to shield myself from the blinding light on the home movie camera.

My mother posed next to me, lifting dresses to the camera, and showing off each gift as boxes flew into the background. Even though there was no sound being recorded, she spoke directly to the camera. "Aren't they gorgeous! Ohhhhh, look at this one!"

She was oblivious to me. Still squinting for vision in the camera light, I bobbed and weaved as the dresses flipped from the box into my face. She did love me, but when a camera was on nothing else existed.

I leaned toward my brother who is eleven years older than me. His outstretched hand tried to protect me. He gently moved each dress as it smacked my face. I could feel his hand on my stockinged knee, assuring me he understood what I was going through.

He glanced back and forth from the camera to me. He did not squint. He was well schooled at being next to my mother on film. He alternated between waving, smiling, and pulling the dresses away from me.

For years I took it personally that my needs were irrelevant to my mother. *Don't you see me? Don't you care about what I want? How could she care more about herself than me? She is my mother! It should come naturally, right?* Wrong.

My grandmother had not taught my mother how to nurture a child. My mother was an improved version, but I still didn't like it. I took her personally. My mother hated what she got. She took it personally. Spoiler alert: *Nothing is personal.*

## Anxiety User Manual: Nothing is Personal

Nothing is personal! Most people, and maybe you, take *everything* personally. A lot of anxiety and hurt feelings come from taking things personally. But please believe me when I tell you that nothing is personal. I learned this from reading *The Four Agreements* by Don Miguel Ruiz. This concept runs throughout the book, and I beseech you to explore the value of this principle if you don't already.

Maybe you're thinking. . . . What??? Is this writer crazy? How do I not take my own mother personally? Here's how we know nothing is personal. My grandmother's behavior was born out of trauma and growing up in the middle of a war; it had nothing to do with my mother. My mother flopping dresses in my face and paying more attention to the camera had nothing to do with me. How could it be personal to a one-year-old child that her mother thought being on film took precedence over connecting with her child? That was my mother's issue. It was personal to her and her desire for recognition and a need to feel special, but not personal to me. There was nothing about *me* that made my mother behave that way.

Let's kick it up a notch. Suppose I am *deliberately* mean to a friend, and she stops speaking to me. Is the fact that she stopped speaking to me personal? No, it is not. It is personal to her. I could say the same cruel thing to three different friends, and they could all react differently. The second friend may stand up for herself, but the third friend might try to get closer to me because she has low self-esteem and feels needy of my friendship. Each different response is personal to the individual having the reaction. Not to me. They react the way they do because of who *they* are, not what *I* say or do.

This concept applies to the good in people as equally as the pain they can cause. If someone lets you into a lane on the freeway, it is not because you're a glimmering soul who deserves to have the sea parted for you, it is because that driver is nice, or at the very least, not in a hurry. If your partner is romantic, it speaks to their character, not yours.

You've probably dated several people. Think about the different people you've dated. You could say something as simple as "Let's eat

Mexican food tonight," and each person you've been out with would have reacted differently.

One might say, "Great! I love Mexican food."

Another, "I hate Mexican food!"

Next, "I don't care."

Someone else, "Can't you be happy with just eating at home? I'm not made of money."

Or even, "I have a better idea. Let's go to Mexico!"

Each person will respond according to their own inner experience. That's how we know nothing is personal. What a person wants to eat, who they want to marry, what makes them angry, and what makes them happy is personal to *them* and their journeys. Even when a person makes a remark that is intended to reflect poorly upon you, it comes from a source within *them*. It is based on their responses and perspectives, not something inside of you. Often, it is based on a reflection or projection of feeling unworthy inside themselves.

Imagine life is a card game in which we are all on the same team. We are each dealt our hand. The idea is to play the card that helps everyone to win. Who is on your team? Let's say it's your partner, your mother, your brother, your boss, and our annoying friend from the cable company. You need a ten of hearts to make your hand better. What if no one has the ten of hearts to give you? Do you take it personally? What if your brother gives you a ten of hearts and no one else does? Does this mean he loves you more than the others do? No. It was just the cards he was dealt.

This is assuming the best-case scenario in which each person knows exactly what you need and want. It's possible your mother has the ten of hearts but has no idea how to play the game, let alone have the insight to give you the card you desire. Maybe your partner has the card but feels underserving of success, so he doesn't play it.

The irony is, even when we are *not* on the same team, we are offended when denied the card we want. Thinking, *what kind of person does that? I would never do that! He has it in for me! Now that is personal!* It is not. It is personal to *them* not *you.*

I am hoping there will be people who love this book; however, there will also be some who dislike it. That is not a reflection on me as the writer, it is representational of the person reading the book. Pablo

Picasso is a renowned and celebrated artist, but some think a five-year-old could paint just as well as he did. That point of view is personal to the viewer, not to the painter.

It would be nice if each person we interacted with saw us clearly and met our needs intuitively knowing exactly what to say or do to create harmony within us. This is an absurd and unrealistic demand! But this is what we expect, and we are wounded when it doesn't work out that way.

Here's the good news. If nothing is personal, then no one can hurt your feelings ever again. They can say or do things that are sad, mad, frustrated, or even happy. But it is because of who they are, not because of who you are. Your feelings as to what others dole out is *your* response, and you can be in control of it. You can *decide* to take something personally, or you can realize that the way a person acts, or thinks, or what they say are indicative of them and their perceptions, and not something inherent in you. Deciding how to respond is your choice. We learned from the last chapter that pausing before responding can be practiced and mastered. That moment of reflection comes in handy when we are taking the words and actions of others to heart. As a therapist I found that taking things personally is at the root of many, if not most problems. Learning this skill will serve you well in all walks of life.

Let's practice how you can apply this concept to yourself and stop taking things personally.

## Build Your Toolkit

Get your user manual.

Use this scenario as a springboard for practicing that nothing is personal.

You are sick of the rain in Seattle despite the fact you grew up there. You put in a transfer to Phoenix. Your fingers are crossed, but how would the following people react to the information?

1. List two family members, two friends, and two coworkers (or casual acquaintances).
2. Next to each person's name write how you think they would respond to your choice of moving.

3. How does that make you feel?
4. Write what it was about them, not you, that may have evoked their response.
5. When you look at it from their viewpoint, with their issues, does it feel less personal?
6. When you know it is not personal, do you feel differently?

# CHAPTER FOUR

~

# Learning to Expect Abandonment

Cars lined up in front of Wilbur Avenue Elementary School with neck-craning mothers seeking their children to give them a ride home. Some kids rushed to their cars. Some kids strolled to get into their mother's vehicle, but all expected their mothers, or at least someone to be there.

I pulled my braid out from under the left strap of my backpack. The gate in the chain-link fence was wide enough for Darren to rush past me as I crossed the threshold onto the sidewalk. I walked past Donelle's mom's car and Lisa's mom's car without looking up. Their mothers were the first in line, as usual. The lineup became more random as I headed down the street, glancing into the occasional car; I made eye contact with moms peering through their windshields for their kids.

My pace quickened as I got halfway down the street. My stares intensified with each car that did not show my mother behind the wheel. I inspected every vehicle, thinking that she could be in a loaner, or a new car, or maybe she sent my grandmother to get me. With each disappointment, my heart quickened its pace. I looked back in the other direction. *Maybe she came from the other way. I should go back to the gate. What if I miss her?* As I ran, I felt my backpack shuttle my dress back and forth. My footsteps were loud. I strained over the car roofs to see if it was her.

I reached the gate and looked in both directions. The cars were thinning out. Within ten minutes, they were all gone. I could see Albert leaning on the fence and waiting down the street. *At least I'm not alone.* Albert's mom pulled up. They drove away.

I succumbed to the idea that yet again, I would be waiting for a while and plopped my backpack down in an effort to protect my skin from the hot sidewalk. As I settled in, I noticed a trail of ants making their way under the fence. I watched them. I hyper-focused on the moving line and the ants began to stand out as individuals. Many of them seemed to run back and forth in chaos, but the line seemed so purposeful. I followed one ant and imagined its story.

"Hey guys, don't leave me!" he yelled to the ants in front of him.

"Hurry up, slowpoke, or we're going without you," they taunted back.

"Waiiiiiiittttt . . . ," he shouted, as he tried to catch up.

The sound of a car coming around the corner interrupted me. I looked up. It drove past. I looked up and down the street, but no more cars. The sky grew a darker blue, and the crickets started their evening serenade.

## Anxiety User Manual: Wounded Child and Learned Anxiety

It's time to introduce you to Wounded Child. I will take some time on this tool because it's important and needs to be understood in all its complexity. It is a construct I created as a therapist to represent the voice of insecurity, fear, trauma, and more. This is *learned anxiety*. Freud referred to this aspect of ourselves as "neurosis." Some use the term inner child, but I find that term can make people's eyeballs roll with annoyance, out of their heads, and out of my office.

First and foremost, Wounded Child has nothing to do with your age. Wounded Child represents the voice of both childhood and adult issues. While the story I shared in this chapter involved a childhood story that contributed to my abandonment issues, I have had experiences as an adult that show up in my life as Wounded Child. For example, I had an employee who tried to make trouble for my company, even though she was unsuccessful, the angst that it put me through triggered my Wounded Child to become fearful when I sensed potential disharmony in the personnel at my clinic.

Perhaps an ex-partner cheated on you and now you have trust issues. Or maybe a car accident in your twenties has left you fearful of driving on the freeway. Abandonment, trust, trauma, and the like can show up anytime and anywhere. Wounded Child is hyper-vigilant, believing everything is a lion. Wounded Child will try to run your life based solely on your scary experiences. It will interpret the world around you and express your needs through a dysfunctional lens of life. The healthy lens through which to operate your life is your Capable Adult Self, who I will introduce you to in chapter 6, but for now, let us get to know Wounded Child.

I can recognize now that my mother's continual pattern of forgetting to pick me up was *not personal*, as discussed in chapter 3; based on that premise, I can forgive my mother and remain unaffected by her behavior. But I need to recognize my Wounded Child's abandonment issues to have healthy relationships in the present day. My Wounded Child has lots of learned insecurities and fear, not just abandonment.

Here are some of the thoughts my Wounded Child has that create anxiety for me: *What if I sound stupid? I shouldn't have said that. She hates me. I'm gonna get fired. What if it all goes wrong? I will fail. I could die penniless. What if I end up alone? Am I a fraud? What if they don't like me because____?*

My Wounded Child longs for connection, but she is also paranoid, insecure, and thinks she's omnipotent. She can send me careening off the cliff of "what ifs" and anxiety-filled doomsday scenarios. For example, when someone seems angry at me, or a person has not read my mind, or if I'm looked at funny, or when someone uses "that tone," or when my husband tells me where to park or . . . you name it. If my Wounded Child is in charge, she is not going to paint a pretty picture for me or anyone else.

Wounded Child tends to leave others responsible for its happiness and well-being. This is not because she/he/they are playing the victim. Fear and insecurity are interpreting the world around them rather than logic and understanding. Wounded Child desperately needs to feel safe, loved, seen, heard, felt, understood, and appreciated. That's all it *ever* wants. There is nothing wrong with that, but Wounded Child is not a good advocate for getting needs met.

To make matters worse, Wounded Child is likely to activate the Wounded Child in others. Unless we are interacting with an emotional ninja, we will trigger the Wounded Child of the person we are upset with, leaving little hope for a solution.

These are some examples of Wounded Child communications:

## Scenario 1

A spouse's partner is late coming home. Having lost her father early in life, when someone is late, her trauma buttons fire. She loves her partner and knows he's probably just running late, but her Wounded Child begins to panic.

The spouse's cellphone died, and he's running late, and he left his charger at the office. His Wounded Child has issues about not being good enough so he is hard himself. When he feels like he has failed, he scolds himself for forgetting the charger and feels bad that his spouse will be worried.

He walks in through the front door, and the Wounded Children go at it.

Spouses Wounded Child: "WTF! Why didn't you call me?! I was worried out of my mind!"

Partner's Wounded Child: "Jesus, I've been working all day; give me a freaking break."

They are silent through dinner and go to bed angry.

## Scenario 2

Two best friends Amanda and Becky move in together. They are excited to be together all the time. Amanda works from home. She doesn't want to make too much noise and bother Becky, so she shuts her door and is invisible most of the day and evening.

Becky's Wounded Child has issues with not being liked, so she thinks she must have done something to offend Amanda. Weeks go by. One evening Amanda emerges early.

Becky: "Wanna watch a show or something?"

Amanda: "Sure."

Amanda is looking at her phone and gets a text message from work.

Amanda: "Oops, I have to take this." She goes back to her room and shuts the door.

Becky's Wounded Child: "This is bullshit, if she didn't want to move in with me, she should have said so." She leaves and goes to her boyfriend's.

Amanda comes out of her room, relieved to sit and watch TV with her friend at last. She looks around, and Becky is not sight. This triggers her abandonment issues.

Amanda's Wounded Child: *Huh, she didn't even say she was going out. That sucks.* She hears Becky come in later that night who goes straight to her bedroom and shuts the door.

If they never learn the tools to access Capable Adult Self, the friendship deteriorates and they go their separate ways, only calling on birthdays.

Wounded Child also thinks it is a mind reader and can hear what you *meant* to say rather than what you actually said. This kind of omnipotence tends to backfire on itself. It's a surprisingly common error to assume what another is thinking without actually hearing any words to that effect.

## Scenario 3

A man who came from poverty works his way up through high finance. His learned anxiety is financial fear. He is not happy in his career, but his main goal in life is to make sure his family wants for nothing. They live an extravagant lifestyle.

His son has never known money issues and has had most stressors in life removed from him by his parents. He is therefore accustomed to a relaxed and easygoing life. He loves playing tennis. College is overwhelming for him. He has self-esteem issues since most of his accomplishments were handed to him on a silver platter. However, he feels empowered on the tennis court and has fantasies of playing professionally, but he would also be content just teaching at the club.

Son: "Dad, I'm just not cut out for high finance, I don't care about the *stuff*. I don't want to go to college. Maybe I'll change my mind later, but right now I really just want to play tennis."

What father hears: "My plan is to die penniless and end up living under a bridge."

Father: "Son, you know I support any choices you make; I don't care if you want to be a garbage man. I just don't want you to struggle. College gives you a leg up in the world."

What son hears: "You are a weak loser with no ambition. How are *you, my* son?"

Readers, this is not an exaggeration. I have seen these kinds of conversations and misinterpretations take place on numerous occasions. This mind-reading dilemma goes so deep that people would swear that's what the other person said verbatim. They do not realize they have been listening with Wounded Child's ears. The real meaning of the conversation never stood a chance because the communication itself was misinterpreted.

All these are Wounded Children running around trying to have healthy relationships. It is very important to recognize your Wounded Child. Knowing the issues that trigger you is essential to managing your anxiety.

## Build Your Toolkit

Get your user manual.

Write down your top five examples that trigger your anxiety. Remember you could have acquired these fears as a child or as an adult. These might be deep fears, or perhaps they only show up sometimes in small ways. Keep adding to this list as you deepen your understanding of your Wounded Child.

Here are some learned anxieties to choose from.

Trust

Abandonment

Not being liked/Not fitting in

Financial fear

Feeling unlovable

Beliefs of being less than

Betrayal

Victim stance

Greed

Paranoia

Grandiosity

Anger

Rejection

Low self-esteem

Feeling unattractive or undesirable

Envy

Feeling unappreciated

People pleasing

# CHAPTER FIVE

~

# The Outcast

My need for inclusion began, on a conscious level, in nursery school. Kids were so mean. Or were they? Was that just my perception? I was desperate to fit in. I remember getting grounded for chucking my embarrassing ABC 123 umbrella into the bushes. *Seriously? The ABCs when I'm in the third grade?* I wanted to die. I knew I would get punished for throwing it away, but I would face my mother's fury over not fitting in at school any day. She did not have understanding or empathy for the struggles a school-aged child might have.

Every day, the giant brown paper grocery bag containing my lunch, with my name scrawled in crayon by my mother was concealed under my coat. Why couldn't I get regular plain sandwiches, like bologna on white bread instead of the stinky, sloppy tuna, or peanut butter and banana that dripped off the thick-cut healthy wheat bread and spilled out of the tin foil when I opened it? I secretly loved them both, but not in public!

I was also the shortest in my class, forever getting picked last for team sports. Still, my knotted stomach prayed that this time would be different and I'd be selected. False hope renewed each time the team captain had a chance to choose again . . . wah wah wah. It was never me.

Every time it came down to two choices. The team captain called out in disappointment, "Fine. I'll take Fat Harriet. You take the shrimp."

Deflated, I followed my team out to the field.

The day I hated the most was Saint Patrick's Day. The holiday when everyone in school was allowed to pinch you. I don't know what the was matter with me, but I *never* remembered it was Saint Patrick's Day until I got to school.

On March 17, 1976, I woke up and put on the brand-new shirt my mom let me get at Marshall's the day before, even though it wasn't back-to-school time. A special event indeed. It was a button-down striped shirt of many colors with a gleaming white collar. I loved it.

There was a spring in my step as I hopped from the car and walked through the gate onto the cracked, tar playground. It was a beautiful day. The sun was shining but it was not too hot yet, and a few pink blossoms were beginning to show on the plum trees.

"Hi, Susan," I called out to a girl who sat next to me in class.

"Hey." She waved.

*She waved back!* Thank God. Nothing was more embarrassing than calling out to someone and not getting a response. It was a good day.

"Ouch!" I heard myself say, pain shooting through my arm out of nowhere.

I turned to see Bobby, "Not wearing greeeeeen!" He shouted and pointed at me victoriously.

OH MY GOD. *Is it Saint Patrick's Day?* I looked down at my beautiful multicolored shirt. So many colors, but no green. A barrage of pinching continued until I got to class. As I walked to my seat, I caught a glimpse of the crayons in an open Tupperware container. I snatched a green one and colored the white collar of my shirt. This would stop the incessant twisting of flesh.

Much to my dismay, the fifth-grade class of Wilbur Avenue did not recognize green added after the fact. The day was awful. I hated Saint Patrick's Day.

## Anxiety User Manual: The *We* Needs the *You*

As the years have gone by, it has come to my attention that most people begin to experience social anxiety around the age they begin school. Why? Our DNA is hard-wired with a built-in need for acceptance. It is fundamental to our survival. Social anxiety and the need for inclusion permeate our consciousness from the get-go.

Since the dawn of man, the act of being cast out has meant certain death. The word "outcast" is literal. Being shunned by the clan and from the cave left us alone in the wild to fend for ourselves. Exile diminished the odds of living to slim or none. There is a biological need to be a part of a group. Not being liked can equal death to the spidey senses in the amygdala. Our emotion centers are on the constant lookout for any threat to our existence. Exclusion can even present as physical pain.

We need each other. We rely on one another's individual strengths. The earliest civilized humans held groups consisting of hunters, planters, scouts, weavers, water gatherers, instrument makers, cooks, midwives, tool smiths, healers, ambassadors, and sages. Even the village idiot had an important standing, I am assuming, since there often seems to be one mentioned. We simply cannot exist without the company of others. We need each other and we need to be needed. Therefore, fitting in, being liked, and having value in our clan are primal.

COVID-19 exposed the rapacious nature that isolation can create on a global level. The break from social obligations was a relief for many at first but that soon wore off. Our "bubbles" were not enough. The minimal contact afforded to us with the people in our lives forced anxiety and depression levels through the roof. People who once loved to socialize found themselves afraid to go out and connect. Who could blame them? The news told them that leaving their houses might kill them or their loved ones. The essential connection with their clan was stripped away. Through the desperate attempt to preserve our physical health, our mental health was sacrificed.

Not many saw it coming.

However, the correlation between isolation and anxiety is not new to therapists. COVID-19 circumstances mimicked the deterioration of the psyche brought on by garden variety general anxiety disorder (GAD). GAD starts, perhaps, with not wanting to travel far. Then before long, a road trip is too much. Parties and social gatherings become out of the question. Soon the five-mile radius surrounding a person's home becomes the preferred stomping ground, with a limited amount of select people for social interaction. Eventually, alone and under the covers feels like the only tolerable option. But connection is vital in sustaining long-term mental health. If your anxiety has separated you from your community, your Wounded Child needs your help to reconnect.

Perhaps you are thinking, *nobody wants to be around me*. Or, *I don't make a difference*. That's not true. You just don't realize the impact you have had on so many people. Imagine the world as a body. Every single cell in a body is important. The cells in the foot are just as important as the cells in the heart. The foot cells can be underappreciated and they are hard workers, they are stuffed in a dark room that is stinky and rarely see the light of day, but the heart cells are not going anywhere without the noble foot cells that carry them from place to place. Each one of us is a cell on this planet and we need each other to create successful lives. Everyone brings something unique to the table that no one else can. This means you, too!

We can confuse being liked and fitting in with not being different. In those age-old clans, if they were all weavers or hunters the clan would not have survived. It is our unique abilities that create our value. There is only one you, and the universe created you for a reason. In our struggle to be like others, our individual gifts can be lost. There is only one you. The *we* needs the *you*.

I'll bet you if I gathered every single person *you* have impacted in your life into one room, it would spill over, and they would fill a shopping mall. There are *thousands* of people you have touched in this world without realizing you have. There might be a check-out person you smiled at one day eight years ago, who didn't commit suicide that day, just because you acknowledged her existence in that one moment. An invisible person suddenly felt seen, simply because you held the door open for them. A phone operator you thanked for his help, and then he smiled due to your acknowledgment. Maybe your family thinks your haircut is outrageous, but your niece thinks you're the coolest person ever. Trust me, you have impacted a plethora of people on this planet, and you don't even know it.

The people in this world need you. You need them, too. There are many ways to avail yourself of human contact but pick ways that resonate with you. That's where you are needed. You can volunteer, do crafts, walk dogs, walk on the beach, coach kids, go to the movies, teach, sit at a restaurant counter, or go sit in the park, anything. There are hundreds and hundreds of people out there who need you, just as much as you need them, so no matter what or how, go find them. I promise you, as hard as it might seem at first, you will thank yourself later. We *all* need to feel needed.

Connection reduces anxiety but connecting looks different for each person. Let's take a look at a few ways you can make a start.

## Build Your Toolkit

Starting small might be your easiest approach.

### General Small Ideas

Call one close friend or family member and ask them to meet you outside your home for a meal. Try and form the habit of having one of these dates at least once per week.

Find places where there are there are like-minded people through websites like meetup.com. These are groups of people that have common interests from knitting to hiking.

### Introverts

You are more likely to strike up a conversation in a venue that makes you comfortable. So, for example, if you like to cook, try a cooking class. Think about a hobby you might have or want to try and find a place where others are doing it.

Start to frequent a café close to your home regularly. You don't have to speak to anyone, but as time goes on the faces will become familiar and they will recognize you as well. This is a great way to plant seeds for budding relationships.

### Animal Lovers

If you have a dog, take a walk in a dog park and strike up a conversation with someone sitting there. Just talking for a few minutes can release feel-good neurotransmitters like serotonin and dopamine into your brain.

Call a local animal shelter and ask about volunteering. Try it a few times. You might find a like-minded community.

There are also cat cafés where you can sit and meet people and pet some kitties.

## Gamers Who Isolate

Coffee and game places are popping up all over. They attract people who prefer to connect through gaming but need to get out of the house for their own good. Find a few and check them out. You don't even have to play anything at first, just hang out and observe. Connecting with just one other person there can be a game changer, pun intended.

## Athletes

Find your team. They are out there and they need you.

Jog in the same area at the same time each day. Faces will become familiar and conversations will form with a simple daily wave.

Go as a single to play golf, you will be put with others, and again, you don't have to engage if you don't want to. It will happen naturally.

## New to a Neighborhood or Town or Need a New Friend Group

Joining a local temple or church is a good way to enter a community if you are at all religious.

Frequent restaurants close to your home. You will start to see familiar faces and strike up conversations.

Read the local paper and attend events that interest you.

# CHAPTER SIX

~

# My Choices?

It was a regular trip to the market:

Eggs, orange juice, toilet paper, cat food, Swanson's chicken pot pie, Swanson's turkey dinner, Kraft mac and cheese, and tuna. I rushed my shopping cart through the frozen food aisle, a staunch temperature shift from the ninety-eight-degree weather I escaped when the automatic doors to the store shut behind me, out of the frying pan into the freezer. The frozen dinners lined the bottom of my cart as I emerged into the juice section. Still cold, but not freezing.

My goose-bumped arm reached for the orange juice. A voice in my head, which I now call Capable Adult Self, stopped me. *Why do you always buy orange juice?*

I answered back, *I don't know. You're supposed to buy orange juice. It's good for you.*

The Capable Adult Self continued its rebuttal, *But you don't like orange juice. You never drink it.*

*Don't I?* It got me thinking. My memory presented a montage of countless tossings of unopened orange juice bottles. The swollen bottles called to me from the back of the fridge. The expiration date confirmed their bloating. Out they went.

My awakening began. *I've been buying orange juice every few weeks since I moved out. And I never drink it. That's like,* my fingers assisted me in solving the mystery . . . *one, two, three . . . six years of unused orange juice! Why have I been doing that?!*

The time machine in my brain blurred and swirled into action.

"Drink your juice, girls!" my mother yelled from her bedroom, down the hall, and across the entry hall to my sister and me at the kitchen table. "It has Vitamin C!"

I screamed back, "Why do we have to? It tastes gross after we brush our teeth."

"Because I am your mother!" The timeless, unfightable response that has plagued children for centuries. We drank the orange juice.

The time machine deposited me back into the market. I stared at the orange juice. I was stuck. What should I do? My focus drifted and I caught sight of the guava juice. I did drink guava juice once in Hawaii. They had it at every breakfast buffet. A thrill of independence shot through me as I dared to consider the options. *Could I buy guava juice instead? Does it have vitamin C?*

The self-seeking Capable Adult voice in my head picked up the conversation, *It's got more vitamin C than the orange juice you throw into the garbage can.*

*True.* I summoned my courage and placed the guava juice in the front part of my cart like it was a baby I was caring for. My stomach had a pang. Was I disobeying my mother? *She would be disappointed.* I was not sure I could trust my choice. My Capable Adult Self rose above my previous programming! I tossed my hair back with a shrug of my neck and moved on with a thrill of defiance.

For the next few market trips, I gave myself the freedom to buy guava juice. Guess what? I threw those out, too. It turned out I just don't like juice. My Capable Adult Self gave me permission to stop buying juice.

## Anxiety User Manual: Capable Adult Self

How many choices do you make daily that are not your own? Are they your programmed choices? The choices of Wounded Child, of your family, your friends, your neighbors? Juice seems like a minor item, but what about your career? Your mate? Where you live? How many of those choices are pure you?

Gather all ye voices and prepare to meet Capable Adult Self. I love this voice so much that I wish you could hear trumpets blaring and see Capable Adult Self walking down a red carpet, humbly waving to adoring fans. So far, we've got Wounded Child who speaks for learned and inherited anxiety, our parent's voices, and in the next chapter you will meet your inner critic.

The voice we need to reach for, the voice that will guide us into the life we desire is Capable Adult Self. Wounded Child has been producing *The Anxiety Chronicles* for many years, but there is a new sheriff in town. Imagine making rational and clear decisions that are not fueled by irrational fear. *You* will be the clear-headed one who sees through the problem and knows how to solve it. Pretty cool, huh? You will *love* your Capable Adult Self, but be patient, this will take some time and a lot of practice to let this voice take control of Wounded Child. True happiness takes work.

Capable Adult Self is your higher thinker, trustworthy caregiver, best friend, and healthy protector. It is your wise, spiritual, sensible, fun-loving rational self, and your best support system ever. Will Capable Adult Self make mistakes? Absolutely. Capable Adult Self will also learn and grow from them. It knows deep down that *there is no such thing as failure, only blueprints for the future*. Capable Adult Self understands that. It will see beyond the limited purview of your Wounded Child and soothe it when it feels like giving up or taking its toys and going home.

If there is a voice in your head that sabotages the life you desire, why continue to let it make your decisions? No one else needs to approve of what you do. It is *you* who must be content with your life.

Let's look at an example of how Wounded Child and Capable Adult Self differ.

Suppose you think it would be a fantastic idea to put a window into your floor so that you could see the earth and roots of your house. *Cool*, you think. You go for it. It looks great. But, in the middle of the night, you get up to go to the bathroom and walk across the window. The glass breaks. You cut your ankle. It's a mess. Was this idea of the window in the floor a failure? No. It is the blueprint for the future. Capable Adult Self knows this and perseveres.

Wounded Child: "Who puts a window in the floor? You're lucky you didn't kill yourself! I'm an idiot, what was I thinking?"

Capable Adult Self: "Let's look for a solution, rather than lament the problem. Put the window back in and put a railing around it."

You put the window back in and surround it with stylish brass railing. It looks even better. In the middle of the night, you trip on the railing and break your nose during the fall.

Wounded Child: "What a waste of money. I'm a failure. I should give up on this stupid idea."

Capable Adult Self: "For some reason, I love this idea. I'm not ready to give up. Let's try plexiglass instead of glass. It is see-through just like glass, but it is safe to step on."

It works perfectly. It looks so great *Architectural Digest* does an article on your living room, and you start a new trend. Each plan gone wrong can lead you to your vision and a bounty of unexpected opportunities.

It's time to become your own parent. It's time to trust your intuition and give it life. It's never too late to let Capable Adult Self take the wheel. Put the misguided, toxic messages and programming in the trunk. You may hear muffled yelling but start learning to ignore it.

To take control of Wounded Child's voice you must learn to recognize it first. I am hoping the exercises in the last few chapters have helped you know how your Wounded Child get triggered—how it thinks, speaks, and behaves—but let's recap. Wounded Child tends to predict doom-filled scenarios. It projects danger, fear, and barriers to connections. It is judgmental, frightened, and defended. It is worried, overwhelmed, and has poor coping skills.

*Wounded Child's voice is important.* Remember it is like the fever that alerts you to your sadness, unhappiness, and discomfort. It must be heard. *But it cannot fix your problems.* For that, you need Capable Adult Self.

Capable Adult Self is rational, loving, and a good problem solver. It is compassionate, unafraid, and open to new things and opportunities. It is always prepared to learn and grow to help you achieve your highest good. Every time you reach for Capable Adult Self and replace the thoughts and behaviors of Wounded Child, you are forming new synapses and neuropathways that will move your anxiety from being center stage to a voice that whispers from behind the curtains, and your

Capable Adult Self becomes the new star of your life. We will focus on ways to access Capable Adult Self throughout the book.

## Build Your Tool Kit

Get your user manual. You are going to continue the practice of replacing negative, fear-filled messaging with helpful and supportive ones. This will reinforce brain activity in giving a voice to your Capable Adult Self.

1. Write down the names of five people who have made you feel unworthy or crushed your spirit. Perhaps it was a teacher, a family member, or someone at work.
2. Next to each name write down a sentence that they said that has stuck with you.
3. Now write a sentence containing what you would have wanted to hear instead. Something a loving and supportive person would have told you to help you achieve your dreams. This does not have to come from a real person. This is what your Capable Adult Self would say.
4. Each time you hear a defeated thought come into your head or fall out of your mouth, stop. Ask your Capable Adult Self what it should say instead and commence to re-wire how your brain thinks. The more you do this, the more naturally it will occur. Soon your brain with go straight to a healthy response all by itself.

# PART II

~

# REDUCE ANXIETY

Part II makes up the lion's share of this book. It follows me from my early twenties until the time that I wrote this book. It focuses on how to have a healthy relationship with yourself as well as with the people around you.

My stories will take you through my experiences with therapy, my battle with drugs and alcohol, and to the opening of my clinic. Then I will explain in detail the holistic methods I employ myself and at my clinic, as they relate to the treatment and recovery from anxiety.

~

# CHAPTER SEVEN

# The Inner Critic

When I was nineteen, my mother, after leaving husband number four who was my age, announced, "I hate L.A.! I'm moving to Mexico, or Canada, or Westlake!"

At least her midlife crisis was narrowed down to one longitude line. My brother convinced her that Vancouver, British Columbia, was the place to go, and they both moved with dreams of becoming landed citizens in Canada.

I never called my brother by his real name. I was taught as a baby, "This is Mommy, this is Daddy, and this is Brother." He played many roles in my life, a parent, a brother, a best friend, and my security blanket. Hand to God, I believed he was Superman until I was ten. When he moved to Colorado, I was only eight; I felt half of my heart tear off and sink into the pit of my stomach as we waved goodbye to him from the curb in front of our house. He flew the coop the moment he was of legal age. It was the first of many places he lived.

Once they moved to Vancouver, my brother spent the next year sending me postcard after postcard of *Farside* cartoons, each expressing his plea that I move to Vancouver as well. "You cannot live in L.A. your whole life. You do not want to be 'one of those people.'" Afraid of becoming "one of those people," I moved.

Leaving L.A. came with a sense of adventure and the dread of anxi-ety. Wounded Child made its argument. *How can I leave the place where I grew up? Leave all my friends? What about the rest of the family? My dad, my aunt, my cousins, my grandparents? How will I support myself? What if I don't get a job? Move close to Ma??? Am I nuts? But I miss Brother so much.*

Capable Adult Self rebutted. *It would be nice to live somewhere else, at least once. I can always come back if I don't like it. I can meet new people. I have always wanted to travel. Vancouver is a nice city. My friends will visit.*

This was my chance to live near my brother again. I could finally take an adventure with him instead of watching him leave. I could be like him, a seeker of new lands, new belief systems, and a new favorite breakfast place. We would listen to Cat Stevens and James Taylor while smoking joints, pondering life, and laughing ourselves to tears.

Big surprise. The change was easier than I had imagined. Soon after I arrived, my brother was invited to a mixer at someone's house for single Jewish people. My brother was too nervous about going alone, so he asked me to join him.

"Sure, why not?" I was excited . . . until the day of the party. As I started to get ready, my joy hit the wall like a freight train and my anxi-ety started to ramp up. The search for the perfect outfit commenced.

*What do I wear? I wonder if it's dressy or casual. I barely own any flan-nel.* I chuckled to myself. I opted to self-medicate before I dressed. In those days, I wasn't much of a drinker. I was a pot smoker. I filled the bowl and snapped a bong load.

*Do people here dress the same for parties as we do in L.A.? Duh, I doubt they'll be wearing taffeta. Just jeans and a cute top?* I pushed the shirts in my closet back and forth on the rack looking for a good one. Nothing grabbed me. I worked up a sweat trying on outfit after outfit. I stripped each ensemble off with frustration and laid potential maybes on the bed. The frustration and anxiety continued to build as the hate for my wardrobe grew. At long last, I acquiesced to a choice and donned the winner of the outfit contest.

Just one problem. I hadn't done laundry in a couple of weeks, caus-ing an inner panic about wearing unmatched socks; worse, one of them had a hole in the toe.

"No one will see your feet, Moron. Who cares?" I said this aloud as I settled on the bed to put them on, stretching the toe on the one with the hole and tucking the flap under my foot as I lowered it into my shoe.

Upon arrival we noticed rows of shoes lined up, just inside the front door. That was how I learned it is a social custom in Canada to remove your shoes when entering someone's home. *Oh, my GOD! My socks! The hole?!!* I grabbed my brother's arm.

A fear-filled whisper spit, "Bruth, I *cannot* take off my shoes! I am not wearing matching socks, and there is a *hole* in one of my socks!?"

"Ooooooo, they will probably throw you out of Canada," he mocked at my dread.

"I'm *serious*," my whisper screaming continued.

Recognizing my irrational fear about the sock, he toned it down, "It'll be fine. You look great. Don't worry."

"Maybe I just keep my shoes on?" I said.

"That'll be worse than the socks. Just deal." His eyes rolled and he took his shoes off.

Cortisol flooded my stomach as I removed my shoes with my sweaty palms. *I should have just stayed home and watched TV. Vancouver is so stupid!* I wanted to die.

I walked my nervous self toward the bar area and grabbed a drink. My heart was doing jumping jacks. I spied an empty spot on the couch by a coffee table under which I could conceal my shameful footwear. I sat down and slid my feet under the coffee table.

I surveyed my surroundings checking out every stockinged foot within eyeshot. Not the most impressive selection. A lot of grayish socks that were once white. Some had pretty flower patterns. I saw a pair of Sponge Bob camouflage socks. *Those socks are hideous.* My covert ops continued. Wait! *His* socks do not match! I squealed inside like I won a game show. I looked at the people who surrounded him, investigating with a discerning eye. *No one else seems to care that his socks don't match. No holes, though.* Then I spotted it. *Victory!!! There's a hole!* A girl in the same group of people as the unmatched-sock man had enough bravery to unabashedly expose her toe through her holey sock.

I could breathe a small sigh of relief, but my feet did not retreat from their coffee table disguise just yet. *I cannot believe I tortured myself over socks. You are just a person sitting on a couch. In all your twenty years, have you ever done anything that got you thrown out of a social event? You have not murdered anyone. People seem to like you for the most part. What is the matter with me? Why do I do this to myself?*

"I'm Doug." An outstretched hand yanked me out of my anxious brain.

"Oh, hi! I'm Laura." My hand returned the greeting.

The evening was lovely, and no one threw me out of the party or the country because of my holey, mismatched socks.

## Anxiety User Manual: Positive Self-Talk

Let me introduce you to your inner critic! Did you know that no one is judging you as much as you are judging yourself? What makes this incessant self-judgment permeate your thinking? Here is what's happening. From the ages of twelve to seventeen, you were flooded with hormones that gave rise to deep insecurities, and the notion that absolutely everyone is looking at you, sizing you up, judging your clothes and your skin, and scrutinizing every single move you make.

This is the troublesome age when we begin to look at ourselves under a microscope and assume others are examining us with the same discernment. Genetic programming strikes again. We must be liked. We must fit in. And now let us add to the equation . . . we must attract a mate.

The realization that we are sexual beings with an intense desire to be attractive to others kicks into fifth gear. Biology drives us to procreate, forcing our attention to examine ourselves with a keen awareness of how others view us. We experience what is known as a "personal audience."

The good news is you are not the only one who has a personal audience. Everyone has their own audience; people are more concerned with how *they* appear than how you appear. You are not the center of everyone's attention, but you are most certainly the center of your own.

Perhaps some of you are thinking, *That is not true, I judge people all the time. I'm not necessarily trying to be mean, it just happens.* If that is so, I will wager that you are extremely hard on yourself, and therefore are hard on others. You are the star of your show and, worst of all, you are also your cruelest critic.

The level at which we judge others occurs in direct proportion to how much we judge ourselves. People indeed judge, however, I have found those who are the toughest on others are the toughest on themselves. The more insecure we are with ourselves the more we judge others.

The opposite is also true. Having compassion for yourself creates space in your body to have compassion for others. If you are kind to yourself and do not judge yourself, you will not care as much about what others think, nor will you spend a great deal of your time finding fault in the people around you.

So . . . if we stop disparaging ourselves, we will stop disparaging others? Bingo!!! Retire from being your worst critic! Open the floodgates of compassion. There is nothing wrong with trying to do your best and giving yourself constructive criticism but being a bully to yourself is Wounded Child's approach to self-improvement.

Unfortunately, many people believe that being hard on themselves is the best motivator. But is it? If a child was at his desk struggling with a math problem, would you motivate him by telling him he was stupid? Would you say to him, "Don't even bother because you will probably fail again?" I hope not. Therefore, don't speak that way to yourself. Berating yourself is not the key to success.

The healthiest approach is to encourage the child with positive statements like, "You're so close, keep trying. Don't give up, you can do it!" This is how you should speak to yourself too.

It takes practice to stop scrutinizing yourself and to believe that you are not being sized up by others. The flip side of judgment is compassion. If you find yourself judging yourself or others, flip it. Find the compassionate angle. Start noticing this critical voice and give it permission to have more compassion and love for what it's like to be a human.

## Build Your Tool Kit

The following exercises will teach you how to retire your inner critic and replace this misguided coping skill with positive self-talk. Get your user manual.

1. Write down the top five statements your inner critic says to you repeatedly.

2. Rewrite those statements with positive messaging.

   Examples:

   Inner-Critic: I'm an idiot. I'll never get this done.

   Replacement Thought: You can do this, be patient with yourself.

   Inner-Critic: No one wants to hang out with a depressed person.

   Replacement Thought: There are other people out there who need me just as much as I need them.

   Inner-Critic: I'm never going to have enough money.

   Replacement Thought: I am on the journey to abundance and will get everything I need and want.

3. Now, I want you to find a picture of yourself as a child. Preferably under the age of eight. Put this picture next to your bedside and every morning when you wake up, promise that kid that you are going to be nice to him today, then do everything within your power to love and protect this little person for the rest of the day. This little person is alive and inside of you. He hears and responds to everything you think and say.

4. Become aware of when you say things to yourself that involve words like dumb, stupid, fat, hopeless, useless, idiot, or loser. Remember that picture you put by your bed. That little person is the one you are judging so harshly.

5. When you hear your inner critic putting you down, reconstruct the thought in a positive way. Be persistent with this kind of thought replacement. It will become second nature as you rewire your neuropathways.

6. Write down five things that you like about yourself in your user manual each day. This will train your brain to find the positive. Make each entry different. Anything from I'm a good listener, to I make good grilled cheese sandwiches. In less than two months you will know one hundred things that are great about you.

# CHAPTER EIGHT

~

# Anxiety Is a Liar
# That Predicts Doom

It was a beautiful spring day. The Hotel Vancouver in the distance reflected the gleaming sunshine, and people bustled on the street below. Some carried their to-go coffee cups, others pulled their wire baskets filled with groceries behind them and many walked along enjoying the rain-free day. The world outside my apartment window was carefree. The world inside my body was gray and hopeless. I didn't care that the rain had stopped. I didn't want to go to the market, and I had already consumed three cups of coffee, evidenced by the grounds dripping across my kitchen sink between the filter and the open bag of coffee.

My sister decided to come to my rescue and picked me up for a short road trip, a day of fun. Vancouver to Whistler, "the sea to sky highway," was the plan. Her car was filled with pot smoke as we hot-boxed ourselves from the get-go. I coughed and tried to hold in the smoke simultaneously—the veins at the side of my head bulged and my eyeballs strained to stay in their sockets as I held in the expanding smoke. I passed the joint back to her.

"We are gonna have fun, Sisu!" she said.

"I know," I choked out, still fighting to keep in the smoke.

While my gaze faced out the passenger window, my thoughts faced inward. I watched the mountain wall as it passed through the gray and dreary atmosphere. I tried to take in the beauty, but my depression and anxiety muted it. Pot didn't have the liberating effects it used to have. My fingers found my temples, and I rubbed them as usual, trying to release some tension.

"What's the matter, Sisu?" my sister asked.

Heavy sigh. "I don't know. The usual, I guess. Work stuff, bills, blah blah blah."

"I thought work was going okay," she said.

"It is. I don't know. My brain hurts."

She was right. Nothing was wrong at work, but I was fretting about it. Nothing was wrong at all, but everything felt uncomfortable. This feeling of panic filled my body, no matter what I was thinking about or where I was. I couldn't stop manufacturing anxiety. My thoughts were bumpers in a pinball machine that took turns lighting up and sounding alarms. My mind knew no other way to engage itself. That pinball shot from one perceived worry to another with no predictability or reason. It never stayed in one place long. It would provoke fear in one area of my life and then ricochet straight to another, rapid-fire, causing me to swirl into a nebulous cloud of dread and doom.

She reached over and pet my hair. "Why do you think so much?" she said in a baby voice.

I didn't answer. I was stuck in the muck of despair.

We continued the drive. I strained to be present. For a moment I caught a glimpse of nature. "It is a beautiful drive. It's weird how bald eagles are everywhere up here, but back in the States, they're practically extinct."

"I know, right?!!" She tried to keep me engaged. "They should call them white head eagles instead of bald eagles."

"True," I answered, nonplussed.

An invisible arm pulled back the spring and shot another pinball out. I was gone again.

"It would be funny if they were called combover eagles." Her attempt at humor fell flat. "Speaking of Eagles, let's turn on some good tunes." She popped in a cassette tape. *Hotel California* started playing midway through the song. My sister sang and then she leaned toward me, miming her hand holding a mic, and queued my turn to sing.

I did not chime in. I pushed on my temples again. My head was pounding. Music was the last thing I wanted. Her "sister sense" picked up on this right away.

"Ok, so not so much with the music." She turned down the song. "Whistler is supposed to be beautiful. We'll smoke it up and have some yummy lunch . . . we'll have a good time up there."

"You don't understand," I muttered. "Everywhere I go, my brain goes with me." That epiphany stuck with me. *There is no distraction great enough to silence the torture.* My obsession with the what-ifs and doom-predicting scenarios was never-ending.

"My brain is not my friend," I said to her.

"Well . . . how do we make it your friend? Maybe we can fix it?" she said with hope in her voice.

"I have no idea," I said. No matter what was happening around me, beauty, friendship, love, or weed, my depression and anxiety were stalwart enemies to all of it. Happiness was an inside job. I would have to become friends with my brain before it would let me enjoy my life. I just did not know how to accomplish that kind of peace. It would take me twenty more years to figure it out.

## Anxiety User Manual: Spiritual Solutions

*Anxiety is a liar that predicts doom.* It is supposed to detect danger, but an overwhelmed limbic system will falsely predict doom. Wounded Child will listen to your anxiety like it is gospel and believe the negative picture it is painting. When your limbic system becomes hyper-vigilant your anxiety will think up the worst-case scenarios and ruin an otherwise seemingly perfect day.

Life is full of wonderful possibilities. I have learned that the true elixir for fear is a spiritual connection. An internal knowing that *no matter what* everything is going to be okay. Iceland is reported to have the happiest people per capita. They attribute their joy to the saying "Þetta reddast" (pronounced thet-ta re-dust), meaning everything will work out okay. To maintain inner peace, we need to know that *no matter what* we will be alright. Knowing how to trust the universe to get me through difficult times eluded me for decades. As my trauma grew it trained me to expect more trouble ahead.

I had no spirituality to help me buoy the storms. I had confused religion with spirituality. I believe most religion includes spirituality, however, not all spirituality includes religion. I was raised Jewish, but I am not religious, plus I love shrimp and pork. I was intrigued by the metaphysical, but when my mother met her fourth husband, aka her soulmate, and started to follow gurus that channeled spirits, I packed my bags, left the house, and checked my spiritual belief system at the door.

Today my higher power of the universe is God. Call it whatever you want, but inner peace is all about spirituality. I want to teach you throughout this book ways to create your conduit to a higher power. A spiritual connection makes the world a safe place to be regardless of the hand life dealt you at any given point. That's not to say your journeys are painless. Death is inevitable, illness happens, financial troubles arise, and, of course, heartbreak. But through it all, everything ends okay. Life still holds so much to enjoy, and my mission is to help you know that on a visceral level.

Mainstream society has taught us to meet our needs. All the other stuff is considered "woo-woo." The holistic approach is a fabulous and effective prescription for anyone wanting to enjoy life. It is particularly effective at freeing those of us who suffer from anxiety and depression, but it gets miscategorized by many as spiritual bullshit. I want to help disparage that myth and shout the virtues of holistic healing from the rooftops.

Let's look at the definition of the word holistic as relates to health. The holistic approach involves looking at the person as a whole and it divides that whole into three parts: body, mind, and spirit. I'd like to break it down even more.

The body is made of several components such as organs, flesh, bones, and veins. If you treat one part of the body, it is felt in the rest of the body—that is, increased blood flow leads to increased oxygen, clearing the nasal passage affects the ears and eyes, and pressure points in the feet can impact many places throughout the body.

The mind was recognized by early Greek philosophers, but the idea of consciousness was brought into the mainstream by Descartes in the

1700s and explored on a more complex level by Freud two hundred years later. It is considered separate from the brain and is attributed with thoughts, ideas, and unique interpretations of the world around each individual.

What makes up spirit? Spirit is described by at least fourteen different definitions! They range from the supernatural, frame of mind, and disposition to slang for booze. Thousands of years before anyone considered that the mind existed, the spirit was part of our self-concept! The earliest cave drawings of primitive man depict spiritual images. Spirituality is an intuitive part of human existence. It is complex, diverse, and ever-present. Even the agnostic or atheist has spent time contemplating spirit. We don't wonder what will happen to our bodies when we die, we want to know what happens to our spirit.

A more applicable concern is, what is happening to our spirits while we are alive? How is your spirit doing today, tomorrow, yesterday? What is bringing your spirit down, or better yet, what is bringing your spirit up? The key to banishing anxiety and depression is lifting your spirit and teaching it to soar. I'd like to help you add your spirit to your toolkit.

## Build Your Toolkit

1. Write down how you personally define spirit.
2. List five ways that help you to connect with your spiritual self.
3. Write a prayer to your source that defines what you want in your relationship with spirit.

Here's an example of what my entry would look like, but don't limit yourself to my example, write from your soul.

### Laura's Connection to a Higher Power

1. Universal Energy.
2. Feeling the wind, doing creative things, meditating, listening to music, connecting with people.
3. Great big Universe, thank you for helping me to understand I am a part of you and you are a part of me. I need your protection and

the lessons I learn through both joy and pain. I am in awe and exhilarated when I feel our connection; those moments of feeling I'm on the right path. I really love the laughter thing! I believe I am here to grow, and I hope that I help others along the way. I am grateful for all the abundance you offer me, the beauty I see in every sunset, the music I hear in every hooting owl, and, oh yes, the chocolate.

# CHAPTER NINE

~

# Conventional Therapy

Samantha was an anxiety therapist. I had seen her on the local cable show hosted by my mother a few months before and I decided to give her a crack at fixing my crazy brain. I was approaching thirty and anxiety still ran my life. She was an attractive petite woman. Nice demeanor. I can still picture the small mole above her lip and her medium-length black hair, just like Mary Tyler Moore. Most of the time my eyes were trained on the giant painting behind her. The background was aqua and there was a giant cartoon globe in the center, but I tended to focus on two turquoise swirls that danced around the animated image of planet Earth.

"I had a panic attack again yesterday morning," I recounted.

She nodded and made a note on the pad resting on her lap.

I went on, "I tried the shallow breathing instead of the deep breathing like you said."

"Oh, how did that go?" Her voice was flat.

My voice indicated surprise as I shared, "It actually worked. A little bit. After that I smoked a joint, but that only helped a little, too."

She waited for more, but when I remained silent she remarked, "It seems that the marijuana works less and less."

I defended my best friend, "Not really. It's the only thing that actually does work. My life is just so stressful, ya know?"

"Did you get any sleep this week?" she queried.

"That would be a big fat no. I mean, I'm sure got a couple of hours dozing in and out, but . . ." There was no need to finish the sentence.

"In better news," I switched the subject, "I'm going on a trip to Hawaii next week. It's last minute, but my cousin invited me to go with him, and I haven't been there since I was five years old."

She continued jotting notes.

"My strongest memory is making a lei with these little white and yellow flowers. They smelled soooo good." The session progressed as it normally did; me jumping from subject to subject. I told her I'd see her when I got back.

I returned to her office after my trip. Her usual poker face disappeared as I walked in the door. "Wow. You look terrific!"

I smiled; my face was still relaxed from the trip. I plopped my ninety-two-pound self onto her couch, my body was loose as I looked down at my feet and slipped off my shoes. *Even my toes are still spread out.* They had enjoyed the freedom provided by the island custom of wearing flip-flops.

"Hawaii was great. It was so simple. Life is so stressful when I'm home, and I get caught up in so much shit, but the truth is, all we have to do to survive is eat and sleep," I said.

Her eyebrows lifted, "That's very interesting."

"How so?" I questioned.

"Because you don't eat or sleep," she remarked.

*Oh my God. She's right.* I kept my eyes focused on the turquoise swirls of the painting as this mind-blowing revelation sunk in. We sat in silence as I began to realize that I lived my life in a manner that deprived me of the most basic human needs. I was an underweight insomniac.

"Damn, you're good," I replied, still in shock. *Holy shit. Therapy works.*

## Anxiety User Manual: Ask for Help

While working with a therapist didn't fix all my problems, this was my first attempt at addressing my anxiety that didn't involve drugs. I wasn't ready to give up my vices and wouldn't for several years to come, but that moment in therapy changed my life. I started eating again. It was hard at first. I had to force myself beyond the half sandwich at lunch and potato chips for dinner routine, but with my therapist's help, I did it. She taught me a few good tricks about anxiety that I still remember and pass on to my patients today, short breaths instead of deep ones during an anxiety attack is one that stands out the most.

I was lucky that seeking therapy was stigma-free in my family, but that's not true for everyone. Many cultures frown on seeking help for mental health, and while that is an obstacle for many, my experience is that the biggest block to overcome is ego. Ego filled my head with thoughts like *I didn't need help*. Or, *I know exactly what to tell my friends when they are upset or in trouble, I just need to figure out how to take my own advice.* Or external obstacles like, *It's so expensive; I don't have the time, I am waaay too busy;* and *How can therapy really help anyway?*

It does. Or at least it can. Let's start by removing some of the afore-mentioned blocks. Ego and self-love are complete opposites. Ego wants to figure it all out on its own, whereas self-love has no shame about doing whatever it takes to feel better. So, if ego is stopping you from getting therapy, summon your self-love to muster up its strength and give ego its imagined obstacles a time out, long enough to at least try therapy.

Even if you give *the* best advice to your friends, it is not that easy to have objectivity about yourself. I knew I was an underweight insomniac since 1996, but it wasn't until Samantha said it, in just the way she did, that I saw from an objective point of view that my subconscious had been depriving me of basic survival needs. A good therapist will see things that appear to be so obvious when it's pointed out to you but remain shrouded in mystery until revealed by a skilled outside observer. That's not to say we can't have insight about ourselves on our own, but it's sure a lot faster with professional help.

Taking care of your mental health can indeed be expensive, but it doesn't have to be. With the benefit of the internet, I'll bet you can find affordable therapy very close to where you live. Maybe your ego is thinking, *Oh, sure, you get what you pay for. I'm not going to some cheap quack.* Many people in the mental health field are not "in it for the money"; they are good at what they do and found their purpose in help-ing others. Keep in mind you don't have to commit to the first person you meet with. You might like the person sitting across from you right away, but if you don't, then try a few people until you find someone you can connect with. Someone who seems like they "get you." I assure you, the right fit is out there. If you can go from place to place trying to find the right shoes or the right car, you have it in you to find the right therapist. I know this proposition is daunting when you are struggling with anxiety, or even more so with depression, but if you got this book, I know you can do it.

Okay, now you've acknowledged it's okay to get help, and you're ready to find the right person. Now there is the question of your busy schedule. There is *always* time for yourself. If you don't know that yet, it's time you did. We know we should put the oxygen mask on ourselves before we go to help others, but chances are your anxiety has directed you to do the opposite.

If someone you dearly loved said to you, "I know you are busy, but I need help getting to this doctor session for one hour every week, my life depends on it and I feel bad asking, but you're the only one who can take me." Would you do it? Would you find room in your hectic schedule? I'm gonna go out on a limb and say you probably would. Be the someone you love dearly and find the time.

Finally, why would therapy help? We all still laugh about my grandmother saying to my father when he went for therapy, "You don't need a psychologist, it's all in your mind!"

If your car is not working properly you don't hesitate to take it to a mechanic, you figure out how to pay for it because you can't get around without it. Well, how are you getting around with anxiety and dysfunctional thinking?

I'll take it one step further. If you are taking good care of yourself, you're trying to stay ahead of physical health. You don't go to a doctor when it's too late. You go ahead of time because you want to stay healthy. Mental health is the same. Stay ahead of the curve. Many physical ailments are the body's response to poor mental health. My eating and sleeping issues were symptoms developed by my body, pleading with me to change my coping mechanisms. Many of my patients come in with stomach pains, or migraines, or sleep issues and they have tried everything under the sun to no avail. By dealing with their mental health the body falls in line. The fish stinks from the head. Keep your head healthy and the body will follow.

## Build Your Toolkit

If you know deep inside you need therapy, why don't you search the internet right this very moment? In your search include keywords like anxiety and depression, and mention low cost or affordable if that's important. Most therapists will list their specialties on their websites, so look for therapists that specialize in anxiety. A common treatment for anxiety is called cognitive behavioral therapy (CBT). This type of therapy helps you to reframe how you think about things. It challenges the thoughts and behaviors brought on by your anxiety. If you have obsessive compulsive disorder (OCD) you might want to focus on exposure therapy. That title may sound daunting, but exposure therapy is a safe and effective treatment for OCD.

For me, mindfulness and learning how to self-soothe are essential to the treatment of anxiety and depression. Find a therapist who understands that and can help you to apply these elements to your healing.

You might think you prefer a male, female, or LGBTQ therapist. This is okay, but don't be too close-minded. You may find you have a connection with someone unexpected—don't limit yourself.

If your issue differs from anxiety—that is, depression, posttraumatic stress disorder (PTSD), or attention deficit disorder (ADD)—follow the same idea. Look for people who specialize in your issues. If you have insurance, your insurance carrier will have a list of therapists in your network and close to where you live. Here are a few sites you can try as well.

psychologytoday.com
Betterhelp.com (online sessions and well-priced; I prefer in-person, but if this is what works, go for it.)
adaa.org
nami.org

If it's appropriate, ask a friend or family member for a therapist they like working with.

# CHAPTER TEN

~

# My Heart Attacks My Brain

"I don't feel so good," I said to my first husband.

"Why don't you go back to bed?" he suggested.

"I don't know." I hated going to bed during the day, even when I was sick. I looked down the hallway toward the bedroom.

"Your call." He flipped to a football game on TV.

My head pounded at the sound of the announcer. I headed down the hallway to the bedroom.

I lowered myself to my pillow. My hand found my stomach, and my palm made a small, gentle circle around my midriff. I lay there trying to maintain consciousness. As I stared blank-eyed at the ceiling, I saw three bug carcasses scattered on the inside of the light fixture. My body felt drained of blood, my face was ashen, my muscles hung thick and heavy. I pictured Roy Scheider having his second heart attack in the movie *All That Jazz*. I could see him lying on the hospital bed pale and sweating. *I feel just like he looked. I'm having a heart attack.* I did not have the sensation of an elephant sitting on my chest; it was more like the elephant was pulling down from inside my chest. Doubt was nonexistent. I reached for the phone and dialed 911.

"911 operator, how can I help you today?" a nonplussed voice said through the receiver.

"I'm calling for an ambulance. I think I'm having a heart attack," I said like I was ordering a pizza.

Her voice did not quicken. "What's your location, ma'am?" I gave her my address.

"I'm sending the paramedics now, ma'am. Is there anyone home with you who can answer the door?" she asked.

"Uh, yes. My husband can answer the door," I responded.

"Ok, just hold tight, ma'am." She sounded reassuring. I continued staring at the ceiling. My mind was blank.

I heard the loud knock of the paramedics. *Jesus, that was fast.*

"We received a 911 call," a muffled voice came through the front door.

"What . . . ?" my husband mumbled in a nap-induced stupor. I heard him shuffle over to open the door as the banging persisted. "Hey. No one called from here."

*Oh shit, don't send them away.* With the last strength in my body, I called out, "I'm back here."

I could hear the paramedics rush down the hallway. *Oh, thank God.* They asked me a battery of questions while hooking me up to different equipment. After a few tests, they strapped me to a gurney and ordered my husband to follow us to the hospital.

At the hospital, the cardiologist repeated the questions asked by the paramedics and confirmed I was indeed having a heart attack.

"Am I going to live?" I asked.

"I'm going to do my best," he stated bluntly.

Seriously? Lie to me! If I die, it's not like I can sue you. Shit.

One hour later, I was in surgery. By 2 a.m. I was in recovery with a stent in my circumflex artery. I get to live and stress another day.

## Anxiety User Manual: Stop Shouldering All over Yourself

The doctors had no explanation for why I had my heart attack. They called it a perfect storm. Whatever the hell that means. Deep inside, I knew exactly why it happened. My life looked great on paper, I finally had the three-bedroom house with a pool, two nice cars, and both my husband and I were respected talent agents who had the privilege of attending Oscar ceremonies. By all accounts, I was a *success*. Nevertheless, inside I was miserable. I was living the dream, so why did it feel like a nightmare? I didn't get the chance to figure out my dream. My true self was unactualized and my inner glow had never seen the light of day.

In my twenties, I used to fantasize that if I got killed or died young, I would never have the chance to fail. People would say, "She had such potential." "She really would have done big things." "Such a loss." I would be remembered as a winner who just never got the chance to grab the brass ring. The pressure would be off, and I would still have arrived. Now here I was, the epitome of what I should be, and I was slowly killing myself. This experience is not unique to me. I see this in my clinic; people coming in who feel lost, or on the wrong track at various stages of their journeys.

With teens, they are under so much pressure to "become." "What is your passion?" "What is your major?" "Your friends are getting accepted at important colleges. What is your GPA?" "What do you want to do with your life?" How the heck do they know? They have not yet had a chance to live in this world on their own, let alone decide the part they want to play in it. They steal moments hiding under dark covers or play video games through the night with fellow commiserators, while their parents worry.

Of course, some never had the chance to pick. People who feel there is no choice for them because of the station they were born into in life. Lower-income kids, who get jobs at young ages to help support their families, focus on survival, which has robbed them of the hope that there are any other options. Depression clouds their experience and they come in hoping there is a rainbow somewhere. They know deep down there must be more joy in life.

Then there are the patients who "shoulded" all over themselves. College done, they now must find a job in the career indicated by "their choice" of majors. Time to get to work. They want to live up to their parents' expectations, or the dreams that they perceive as their own. The pressure to find a job is overwhelming. They do not seek their interviews with gusto but with dread. They can't understand why they aren't excited. They can't sleep. They overeat or under eat, and report having nausea or other abdominal pain.

I ask them, "What is it about your life that you can't stomach? What is your body trying to tell you?"

If they continue into their thirties and forties without listening to their bodies and addressing inner happiness, they develop ulcers, eat antacids, and take antidepressants and sleep aids. Their social lives disappear. The relationships they have managed to sustain have become strained.

The most "should on" people are the ones who have dragged themselves through the scenarios described earlier and still have no idea who they really are. Their kids have grown, and they are so overwhelmed with hyperbolic concern about their newly launched offspring, that they don't know what to do with themselves. Or they never had kids and are burnt out from their careers and jobs. They are balls of anxiety with no sense of what gives them purpose or pleasure. They haven't had the chance to find out their true desires and find themselves asking, *What's it all for?*

Whatever your age, if you are reading this book, you understand how that question feels. Deep down inside there must be something more to life, or at least you hope so. You are right. It is your birthright to live the sublime experience of self-actualization.

A psychologist named Abraham Maslow proposed that life was like a triangle made up of five categories. Let's start at the bottom of the triangle and work our way up.

Physical safety: air, food, shelter, water
Safety needs: personal security, health, employment
Love and belonging: friendships and a sense of connection
Esteem: self-respect, recognition, freedom, status
Self-actualization: feeling of becoming the most that one can be

The higher up the triangle one goes, the more connected they become with their soul's purpose. For most of my life I lingered between two and three. It wasn't until my forties that I began my journey further up the triangle. I had no idea what self-actualization was but somehow my soul knew. My anxiety and depression were my body's way of guiding me to find my true purpose.

Part of life is honoring commitments and taking care of business, however, the pathway you choose to get your needs met is up to you. Nobody else gets a vote. I fulfill my responsibilities today but on my terms. My heart and my gut are in charge of my brain now, instead of the other way around.

This is your opportunity to explore child-like wonder and release yourself of the "shoulds." It is your time to give yourself permission to start discovering the real you, and a life of contentment that is unique to you and you alone.

## Build Your Toolkit

Get your user manual.

1. Write down each of the following categories:
   Career:
   Mate:
   Town you live in:
   Type of house/apartment/condo:
   Home décor:
   Music choices:
   Friend choices:
   Future plans:
2. Now fill in your current answers.
3. Repeat the categories and write the answers that you really want. If they are the same as your first answers, that's terrific. If they are different, create a vision board that depicts the changes you want to make and hang it where you can see it every day.
4. Let's make a vision board! Trust me on this. I have made several vision boards and the images I put on them have come to fruition. Even writing this book was something I put on a vision board. You are setting this vision into action by creating energy around it and drawing it to yourself in the quantum field. We will learn about the quantum field in the Re-Creation portion of this book. Not only are you generating energy for these visions, but you will also reinforce this message every time you look at

your vision board or even pass by it without looking. This is not woo-woo; this is science.

If you have never made a vision board here's how: Get a blank poster board and cut out magazine pictures that contain the visuals of what you desire and glue them onto the poster board. You can cut out letters or words, such as PEACE, NATURE, SUCCESS, MONTANA. You can also add them on your board. Glue flowers onto it. Be creative and have fun with it.

# CHAPTER ELEVEN

~

# Going Off the Deep End

Judge Judy slammed down her gavel. "I don't think so, Sir! You will give your ex-wife the money you owe and figure out how to live your life like a responsible human being!" It was 12:30 in the afternoon, and I was still in bed. It wasn't my bed. It was my cousin's dead grandmother's bed. My post-divorce move to Hawaii to drink, screw, and hula had not proven to be the elixir I had imagined. I was back in Los Angeles; if hell was limbo, this must have been hell. I lay in bed. I didn't shower anymore. Clad in my ex-husband's old boxer shorts and an oversized stained white t-shirt, I went to the edge of the pool in the backyard. I stared at the bottom of it. I wasn't shaking anymore because I had swallowed the last ounce of vodka left over from the night before to stop my morning withdrawal. I figured I might as well freshen up while I waited for my morning delivery of booze and deli food.

The pool water was still, and I could see where the patches of the black bottom had worn away. I let myself fall into the deep end. The water made my face feel alive. I could feel my eyes strain through the chlorine as they opened to take in my surroundings. It was quiet down there. I watched the bubbles pass from my mouth to the surface. I could hold my breath for a while. I stared at the blurry sky for a bit and then my arms spun me into the swimming position, and the t-shirt swirled gently around my body, comforting me like a loose swaddle. *Am I a baby? This is no rebirth. I'm barely alive anymore.*

I was running out of air. I could feel the sun in my eyes before my head breached the surface. I took a breath and commenced bobbing.

The pending visit from my father later that day popped into my mind, and dread crept into my stomach. *Shit. I better hide the empties. I'm going to have to get dressed too.* I hated for him to see me like that. The thought of it was depressing. The fresh feeling of the water was gone. I crawled out of the pool, stripped the wet clothes from my body, and draped them across the hot cement to dry. I stared at the clothes on the ground. *My body feels so much heavier on land.* I walked back into the bedroom and flopped down on the time-worn mattress.

The red numbers on the digital clock read 12:52. *Where the fuck is Gil Turner's Liquor?* The Sunset Boulevard landmark had been supplying alcohol to Hollywood hopefuls, musicians, and underaged teens with fake IDs since 1953. Thank God they delivered. *I guess it's only been thirty-five minutes.* I had placed my daily order of Smirnoff's. I'd lie to myself and order the 750 ml bottle hoping that I would make it last longer. But I knew I'd drink the whole thing sparing just that little bit at the bottom for the next day and then call for my next delivery.

*Greenblatt's should be here by now, though. I should call them and complain.* I didn't have the energy. My onion bagel with lox and cream cheese would be there any minute. *I'm barely going to touch it anyway.* I would need the alcohol to follow immediately, to preclude the nausea created by the tiny bit of food I might have choked down. I hadn't been able to stomach an authentic meal in months. *I'll smoke a bong if the booze takes too long.*

A genius thought rushed into my head, and the idea made adrenaline flood my body. *I'll ask Dad to bring me Xanax!!!* Renewed life entered my body. The future felt brighter as I reached for the phone. But feelings aren't facts.

My father answered, "Hi, darling."

"Hi, Daddy," I answered back. I had turned on my nervous voice. "I am so sorry to ask you, but I'm so stressed about finding an apartment, and I really had trouble sleeping last night."

I could sense his discomfort through the phone by the sound of his body shifting in the background; then a slight, audible moan moved through his throat.

"Will you please bring me a Xanax when you come over? Please?" I begged.

There was a pause, but I knew he would give in. His disappointment revealed itself in his tone. "Okay, sure, sweetheart. Do you need anything else? A turkey burger from Marty's?"

"That would be great! I love you sooo much."

"I love you too, Blacky." I could feel his love through the phone when he uttered his lifelong nickname for me. It is far louder than any disappointment. He had chosen to call me Blacky, because when I was born my hair was so blonde. Always with the humor.

*He's the best.* "See you soon. Can't wait," I said.

"Me too, darling." He hung up.

As I put the phone down, I released a big and loud sigh of relief. I flopped back down on the bed and let the wet sheets cool my depleted body. The second I lay down, the doorbell rang. I was hoping I looked like I just got out of the shower to the delivery guy. I opened the door.

"How are you doing today, Ms. Rhodes?" he said in a much too chipper fashion.

*What the fuck are you so excited about? You're a delivery boy at the age of fifty-something.* I could hear how obnoxious I sounded in my head. *God, you're such a bitch. At least he has a job.*

I put on a fake smile. "Great! You're so awesome. Thank you so much!" I signed the visa slip and traded him five dollars for the paper bag full of Jewish soul food.

"No problem. See you tomorrow?" he winked.

*Fuck you. You don't know me.* "Could be!" I forced a half-smile and closed the door. The grin crashed off my face the second the door shut.

It was now 3 p.m. The vodka and the three bites of bagel sated me temporarily, but now the anxiety about having to brush my teeth and get out of bed had set in. I had been perseverating about it for the last half hour. It ached my body and brain. You'd think I was about to be executed. The depression of facing my father dripped through my thoughts, creating a paralyzing, dense fog. *Remember, Dad's bringing Xanax.*

By the time my dad rang the doorbell, the empty vodka bottles were back under the bathroom sink. I had dressed in sweats and a clean t-shirt. I knew it was clean because I smelled the armpits. I didn't make the bed. That would be over the top. I opened the door. His Stan Laurel smile stretched from ear to ear. No teeth showed. He was glad to see me. And I him. The truth is, I had never stopped needing my daddy. *I hope he remembered the Xanax.* I eyed his pocket with my ineffective x-ray vision. We hugged, which was better than any Xanax. The smell of his cologne comforted me, and I melted into his arms trying not to cry.

My despair uttered, "I love you so much, Daddy."

After he ate his lunch, my father's inner camp counselor suggested, "Hey! Let's go for a walk!"

*I'd rather hammer my toes for the next hour.* I knew he was gonna make me do it anyway. But I looked away, hoping to dodge his exuberance.

"It'll be good for you. Come on." He nudged my leg.

"I know. Okay," I said with all the enthusiasm of a dental patient.

The driveway at the house was steep, long, and winding. Going down wasn't so bad. The occasional shade of a tree was a relief from the hot sun. We walked around the park situated across the street. I could only make it about five minutes before I started to feel weak and nauseous. Unknown to either of us, I had both liver and pancreas poisoning.

We started the walk back to the house. I got about fifteen feet up the driveway and couldn't make it another step.

With deep concern, my father spoke, "This isn't normal, Blacky. There's something wrong if you can't make it up a driveway. I think I should take you to Cedar's."

The panic started. *I have to at least smoke a bong before going to the hospital. Fuck!* "I . . . " I knew I needed to say yes. Staying stuck on the driveway or going to the hospital seemed to be the only option. I would not remember how I got to the hospital that day until I had been sober for five years.

## Anxiety User Manual: Addiction—Sometimes We Meet Our Needs Tragically

I'd like to use this part of the anxiety user manual to address addiction.

This story I just shared was the result of living my life with Wounded Child in the driver's seat. I tried stopping my anxiety with drugs. Pot, pills, and the occasional acid trip helped me find peace and connection to the universe for brief and fleeting moments, providing a respite from the uncomfortable person inside. An outsider who didn't really fit in.

People often think of substance use as an escape. I believe it is the opposite. When I was drunk, the music was great, the food tasted terrific, and "I love you, man" was much easier to say. I was in the moment. When I ate a spoonful of Rocky Road ice cream, I was thinking about getting a marshmallow into each bite and feeling that cold, smooth chocolate on my tongue. My anxious brain was put on mute. I didn't care about my heartbreak, my problems at work, a test, or my taxes. All my problems were gone because I was in the moment.

But the second the ice cream was gone, or the joint was finished, or the booze wore off, my thoughts continued their torment. We are not taught how to self-soothe. Healthy habits might inadvertently get picked up along the way, but we are spoon-fed unhealthy coping skills from day one. In movies and on television, when a character is stressed out, they pour a drink, smoke, shop, or eat chocolate. That's what we are taught to do.

Addiction has at long last been recognized as a mental illness. In my experience, one is never cured of this disease, but recovery is without question achievable and sustainable. For now, however, I would like to focus on the disease itself.

Addiction is the only disease that will tell you that you are not sick. Addiction has a voice that lives inside your head convincing you of the opposite. *You are fine. You don't need help.* It will tell you that it is your only friend, that without your substance of choice, be it alcohol, drugs, food, sex, or gambling, you will be miserable. And you believe it. You believe that removing this vice from your existence would ruin it, make it unbearable, make it impossible to get through hard times and good times as well. It tells you that it will meet your needs and make your dreams come true.

Addiction paints a romantic picture of the two of you together. It floods your mind with images of dinners and parties made glamorous by a glass of champagne, nights of pleasant and relaxing sleep because of that magic pill, evenings on the couch together eating chips and ice cream in front of the TV, that will end all of your problems. If you have an addiction or know someone with an addiction, you understand exactly what I'm talking about.

Addiction tells you to keep going when doctors tell you to stop. It lowers the bar as you make excuses for it. It convinces you that you won't get a DUI or hurt anyone. It encourages you to meet lower companions for evenings that will leave you feeling like shit later and destroy any good relationship you might be in. It coaxes you to the pantry, when your stomach is full, and tricks you into thinking there is room for more. It tells you to ignore the awful feelings and self-loathing you will have in the morning because tomorrow it will be different. Tomorrow is never different, only worse, but you listen to it anyway.

Addiction doesn't care if your liver is failing, if your marriage is falling apart, if you're going to go broke, if your pant size goes up year after year, or if your family and friends worry about you night and day. It doesn't care one bit that you could die. It has a life of its own and your well-being stands its way.

Addiction is a tragic way of trying to meet your needs. It is a spiritual hole in your soul, which is trying to fill a heartbreaking and lonely void with anything that takes away that empty feeling. Nothing addiction suggests to you works on the genuine issues. It works for the moment, and then it's gone. The emptiness is back, and it's there forever, unless you decide to get help and end this terrible disease once and for all.

In my personal experience the best way to find freedom from addiction is a twelve-step program, so let me dispel any myths or reservations you may have about these programs and share with you why they work. Let's start with the absurd notion that twelve-step programs are a cult. That is patently not true. You can come and go as you please and there is no crazed leader to follow. Perhaps people think it is cult-like because the word God is used in the program. But I repeat, it is *so not a cult*.

This brings me to the most common reason people reject the program with contempt before investigation. A lot of people believe Alcoholics Anonymous (AA) is a religious organization since it adopted its principles based on the Oxford Group which was religious. But the founders of AA recognized the bad taste religion can leave in the mouths of many and created a program that is indeed spiritual, but not religious.

What's the difference? Religions ask you to follow their prescribed religious leader and that leader's tenets. Spirituality makes no such requests. If you choose to find your higher power in religion, that's okay too. The universe and nature are where I find my spirituality. When I see a sunset the words "Oh, my God," simply float off my lips.

Ironically, when you are spiritually bankrupt, as is the case with addiction, a spiritual program is the last thing you want, but it's the only solution that works. So, if the "God" thing is keeping you away, ignore those thoughts and try it anyway—it's your best option.

I did my thesis based on the idea of a twelve-step program for well-being. I have included the link in this footnote in case you are curious enough to read it,[1] but I can sum it up for you here.

The theories of Carl Jung, Viktor Frankl, and Martin Seligman are inherent in many of the steps. For example, Viktor Frankl, a holocaust survivor, and philosopher created logotherapy. His theory proposes that the meaning you assign to your experience can change how you feel about it, giving you a new lens on your life. Martin Seligman is the father of positive psychology, a philosophy that helps you find solutions to your dilemmas rather than focus on problems. You will find Carl Jung in the steps as they ask you to create self-awareness and identify the different parts of self.

In addition to psychological principles, the very first entry in the basic text of *Alcoholic's Anonymous* is written by the doctor of a medical facility who had failed repeatedly in treating addiction but saw great success in the patients who created and practiced AA.

The steps work because when examined closely, they are based on several sound and evidence-based psychological therapies, put together in perfect order. The following description of the twelve steps is my interpretation of what they are made up of and why each step works.

Step One: The admission that you have a problem, and we all know you can't fix a problem unless you can recognize you have one.

Step Two: Asks you to acknowledge your dysfunctional behavior and realize you need something bigger than yourself to aid you in your recovery.

---

1. https://scholarworks.calstate.edu/concern/theses/4j03d311v?locale=de

Step Three: A commitment to do the steps and let a higher power guide you in changing your behavior.

Step Four: Make an inventory of all the incidents in your life that gave you anger and resentment, find your part in it, and then uncover the fear underneath it. Remember from earlier, always under anger is fear.

Step Five: Share step four with your sponsor. That person will help you identify your part and the fear under the anger, which is not easy to do on your own. They will also share their own fears and anger. This will bond you with your sponsor and help you understand you're not the only one who has deep-seated anger and fear and you're not unique in your dysfunctional coping skills.

Step Six: Helps you uncover how you get in your own way.

Step Seven: Guides you in letting your higher power get you out of the way.

Step Eight: Make a list of the people you have hurt in your life.

Step Nine: You and your sponsor will figure out a way to forgive yourself for any regret-filled behavior and ask others to forgive you, too.

Step Ten: Daily repeat of step four. At the end of the day, look at where you may have stepped on another's toes, and make it right before it festers for either of you.

Step Eleven: Meditation and regular communication with your higher power.

Step Twelve: Get a sponsee and do for a newcomer what your sponsor did for you.


In this book, I am hoping to connect you to your higher self and spirituality.

Do you suffer with addiction?

If the answer is yes, go to the toolkit in this chapter. If you are not sure, then the answer is yes, go to the toolkit in this chapter. If the answer is no, perhaps you can share this chapter with a person whom you love who does suffer from addiction.

## Build Your Own Toolkit

Sobriety is the hardest tool to pick up, but it is a tool that will change your life for the better in ways you cannot begin to imagine. That sick feeling in your stomach will go away and you will be free by using these tools right now.

AA is free and there are meetings near you at all times of the day and night. There are also twelve-step meetings for marijuana, cocaine, and narcotics. There are over two thousand twelve-step programs that address all kinds of issues. That is how well it works. I find AA is the easiest to find, with the most diverse population and most members in there have plenty of experience with other drugs as well. These numbers are local to the United States, but you can search online for AA anywhere in the world and find meetings.

Call Alcoholics Anonymous Hotline: 866-210-1303
Search the internet for AA meetings near me.
Call someone you trust and ask them to help you find treatment.
Hazelden Treatment (they take most insurances): 877-793-5205
Over Eaters Anonymous Hotline: 505-891-2664
Gambler's Anonymous Hotline: 800-522-4700
Crisis Hotline Numbers; SAMHSA National Hotline (treatment locator; this number can help you with any addiction or mental health issues): 800-662-4357

# CHAPTER TWELVE

~

# The Universe Sent a Cat

Hazelden Treatment Center was nestled in the small town of Newberg, Oregon. The outside was painted gray with white trim, and half-dead lawns separated the buildings, but the trees, oh my God, the trees. Autumn in Oregon was picturesque, sweeping the crayon section from peach to burnt sienna with a hint of ripe banana. The air was delicious, crisp, and fresh as a York Peppermint Patty. Los Angeles weather doesn't even know it's fall until November.

On the third Friday of my stay, I took my usual walk from the cafeteria to the main house. They were the only moments of the day I got to be alone. Most of the time, I was in the company of the other patients, feeling miserable and drained. I know this because we had to write a "feeling" word at the beginning of every group, so five times a day, I wrote "drained."

As I ambled along on this particular Friday evening, I thought, *It's so weird being here. Me sober, what a joke. At least it's movie night.* A small treat before bedtime, and then off to try another attempt at sleeping on the plastic-covered bed and pillow. The pillowcase crinkled a cruel reminder in my ear that my life plan had gone seriously awry. Ugh. Still unbelievable. Not quite the lap of luxury and well-being I had been aiming for.

As I walked, I mused, *I wonder what we'll watch tonight. I hope it's a comedy. Whatever it is, it'll be about addiction.* Those are the only kind of movies we were allowed to view. I was trying to walk fast enough to beat the others and snag an end seat between the potato chip crumbs and the arm of the sofa. *At least now I know where all the pleather couches from the eighties went.*

I passed Elenore in the hallway. This was not her first attempt at sobriety, more like her twentieth, evidenced by the fact that at that moment she was mistaking the towel cart for a copy machine. She hadn't redone her fancy updo since she checked in, and now it had deteriorated from the Oscar runway look to hair that was styled with an eggbeater.

I gently refocused her by moving her shoulders away from the cart, "Why don't you head down the hallway that way, Ellie? I think they can help you in the office." I wasn't even sure she knew what I said, but she went in the right direction. *There goes a damn good example of why I should stop drinking.*

I continued to the living room and made it in time to grab a corner seat. The movie started. I had seen this one. It was titled *The Dream Team* with Michael Keaton and Peter Boyle. It was still hilarious. I was laughing. Until I wasn't. Its humor faded as it started to dawn on me. *This movie isn't about sobriety!* My palms began to bead. *This is about people in a nuthouse! An actual nuthouse!* My pulse quickened, and my mouth started to dry up. *Why are they playing this for us??? Am I on a crazy farm?! For real?! Is that what they think?* My heart started to race. The movie played on, but I couldn't hear the words anymore. The only thing I was hearing was my heartbeat. My anxiety pistons were cranking up, and my ears rang, as I wiped my sweat-drenched handprint from the armrest. The gravity of the moment and where I was started to sink in for the first time. *I'm in a fucking looney bin. Rehab is for mental patients!!!!*

As my heartbeat faster and louder, my Wounded Child jumped to the thought of an Ativan. I had managed to sneak one in. The admissions team had taken away my shampoo and watercolor paint set, but they somehow missed the anxiety pill in my wallet. In hindsight, I know the universe planned that.

My roommate Monica noticed my escalating panic. "You okay?"

I didn't make eye contact. My neck was frozen in place. "I don't know," my voice cracked.

She pulled my arm, and we went into the hallway. She just looked at me, waiting for me to speak.

I finally broke the silence, "I think I'm having a panic attack." My hands moved across my moist forehead. "What if I have another heart attack?"

She folded her lips inward as she clenched her teeth. "Fuck, do you think you're gonna have a freakin' coronary?"

We were quiet as my hips darted from side to side with nervous-looking-like-you-have-to-pee energy. I wanted to tell her about the Ativan and ask her if she thought I should take it, but I also didn't want to throw my Hail Mary in the toilet. What if she reported me, or even worse, what if she took it herself? *That would suck for both of us.*

Above the percussion of my heart, the voice of Capable Adult Self rose in the back of my head, "Laura, you didn't come all this way to cope with your anxiety by taking a pill."

I hesitated and stood there.

"This is above my pay grade, man," Monica said, "you should go to the nurse's office."

I couldn't get any words out, but I nodded, letting her off the hook. I turned toward the hallway I had pointed Elenore down only twenty-five minutes ago. I felt as off-kilter as she looked when I watched her staggering across this same carpet. *Am I losing my mind? Is Elenore my future?!* Panic coursed through every cell in my being as I walked down *The Shining*–like hallway.

The fluorescent light in the office nauseated me. I spied Caroline in her chair. Sweet lady. Heavy set, white short puffy hair, clad in worn-out pink pants and a t-shirt that quoted "The Serenity Prayer." Even in a panic, I found the sentiment to be annoying.

She had a slight Georgia drawl, "What's up, honey? You doin' all right?"

I heard a cartoon-sound gulp wash down the lump in my throat as I hesitated to speak.

"It's okay. You can talk to me. That's what I'm here for." She waited.

I needed her to understand the severity of this moment for me. My hands were shaking, and my legs were well-done spaghetti. "I think I'm having a panic attack." A calm voice spoke while my insides screamed like a horror film victim.

She cocked her head to the side and gave me a look I interpreted as pathetic, stupid, pitiful. "Have you tried talkin' to yer higher power, doll?"

*Oh no, she didn't.* I wanted to slap her. My eye-rolling system engaged. I tried to be polite to this inconsiderate and clueless response, but what did I expect? I was in a twelve-step program facility.

"I don't believe in that stuff," I replied.

"Really?!" She exclaimed as if I shared that the Earth was flat.

"Yeah, sorry," trying to hide how annoyed I was at this very moment.

As I fluctuated between panic and frustration, she raised her terrier-like eyebrows, "You mean there is nothing on God's green earth that isn't more powerful than little ole you?"

*I'm pretty fucking powerful. Do you know who you're talking to?* Then Ego made a shocking move and stepped aside for a moment. My mind went to nature. "I mean, I guess . . . nature . . . a forest," I stammered.

"Well, why don't you go outside n' speak to nature?" she suggested.

I thought to myself. *Well, maybe I could stare at the sky and see some stars. I can't stand talking to her. I've got to get out of here.* "Okay, thanks," I forced a smile through exasperated lips.

I headed outside to the back porch. The chill in the air caught me off guard and shook me out of my head and into the moment. I watched my breath form in front of me as I exhaled. I crossed my arms around myself for warmth. The wind blew my hair back as I gazed up at the sky. Clouds. No stars. Just clouds. *Great.* I would have been mad if I weren't so overwhelmed. *What am I gonna do? What the hell is wrong with me? How is this me to begin with?* I started to cry. My face shifted downward, shielding itself from the cold. I shook my head at the wood-slat porch. *Oh God, please help me. I can't do this anymore.* I crept onto the swinging bench behind me and sobbed. I wept in between gut-wrenching wails.

At some point a cat jumped onto my lap. I had no idea where this cat came from, but I started petting it. It started purring, so I kept stroking its soft fur while I drenched the poor creature in my tears. It didn't seem to mind. It just purred away. Several minutes had passed when I heard myself take a deep breath that shuttered me. The petting continued, accompanied by the soothing motion of the cat's paws kneading my jeans, and then all of a sudden . . . there I was. No anxiety. It was gone. Only feelings of calm and peace.

That was my moment. *Wow.* Fear left my body without drugs for the very first time in my life. I sat in awe. All I could hear was the sound of crickets. No drumming heart. No screaming inside. Just a stillness I had never experienced. The cold on my face was cleansing. I watched my breath again. I could sense true peace throughout my being. *This is wild.* I scanned myself to see if panic was about to strike up the band, having only taken a break. But no, my body was serene. From that moment on, I was never the same. And the fantastic thing was, I only wanted to see some stars. In their place the Universe had sent me a living being. A feline healer. Tomorrow my feeling word would be "hope."

I have never craved a drink or drug since. I learned that night there is *something* out there that is connected to me. It's connected to all of us because we are a part of the Universe and vice versa. We are one.

## Anxiety User Manual: My Spiritual Awakening

My connection to this source has grown over the years, ever evolving into a deeper relationship and understanding. I have learned that I can change how I connect with the universe. I can alter my energy just like I can change a radio station, and then I'm hearing a much better song on a much more pleasant channel—goodbye K-SHIT and hello WKR-PEACE. *Everything* is energy. The surface you're sitting on, the format in which you are reading this book, the shirt you are wearing are pure energy. The color red is different from the color blue because of its wavelengths. *All* waves of energy.

You know those days when you rush out of the house and your sleeve catches on the doorknob, forcing your coffee cup to fly out of your hand onto the floor? Then you bang your head on the door trying to clean it up. You finally get on the road, but now you are late and some jerk cuts you off on the freeway, Siri is misinterpreting every other word you say, and the rest of the day is just lousy. You are having one of *those* days.

Then there is the kind of day when as you're getting dressed, you reach into your pocket and find a five-dollar bill. The sun is shining, the salesperson at the store scans a coupon for you for no reason at all, and every song on the car radio is great. It's one of *those kinds* of days!

Nothing in your life has changed, it's just another day, but every-thing has changed. Here is why. We travel in different frequencies, on different waves of existence all the time. Until I was sober for a while, I had no idea of how much I was in control of my vibrational world.

As a therapist, I have come to understand that even though we all live on the same planet, each of us lives in a different world. Think about it. Take your parents, your best friend, and a difficult coworker. Do they live in the same world that you live in, or are their perceptions, their experiences of life and its events quite different than your own? Some see the world as a terrible and scary place. Yet others, who live on the very same block, in the very same town see the world as wonderful. Everyone is on a different frequency, and therefore they encounter cir-cumstances based on the dimension they are traveling in. In *my world* spirituality involves science; magic that is created by the universe.

I had already prayed to the universe for years, "Oh God, please let my pot guy be around." If he wasn't, I still managed to manifest weed, no matter what. I was on the same frequency as the other smokers. I could go to a nice business lunch and boom, the person I was with would offer to smoke a bowl with me in the parking lot. I didn't look at all like a stoner, but my vibrations were loud and clear to other stoners. No one offers to smoke a bowl with me anymore. I look the same. Well, my hair is more gray, but my energy has changed. Except for old friends and some family, everyone I know, and meet are people who do not get high, whether they are sober or not, it's just not on their wavelength.

People tend to rely on their five senses to help them interpret the world around them. They don't doubt their five senses. If a person burns their hand on a hot stove, they recoil and are purposeful in never doing that again. They do not wonder five years later if they imagined it or if it really happened. It is the truth.

Why are spiritual experiences different? You have probably had at least one cool, unexplained event that occurred in your life when you couldn't believe the *coincidence.* Or a "woo-woo" experience that later made you wonder, *Did I imagine that?* You did not. There is so much of this universe that goes undetected by our limited five senses. Did you know that we can only see a small percentage of the light spectrum?

We don't see cellphone waves or microwaves flying around the room. Our sight is limited. Dogs smell things that our noses cannot detect. Deer do not see red or orange, to them it appears green. There is so much happening around us that we simply cannot detect with our five senses, so why limit our belief systems to them? Einstein believed that we understood a pinky nail of what was happening around us.

We sometimes refer to our sixth sense, but we probably have a lot more than six. As my understanding of my higher power has grown, my ability to generate the life I desire has become much more powerful. So will yours.

## Build Your Toolkit

Try changing your own frequency. This is Vibrations 101. There will be more methods as the book unfolds, but this is a good place to start. Multiple studies have shown feeling gratitude is one of the easiest ways to reduce anxiety and depression. Gratitude is also a great way to change your frequency.

Get your user manual.

1. Check in with your body and write down a number on a scale of one to ten that indicates the amount of peace and joy you feel in your body at this very moment.
2. Write down the name of someone that you love very much.
3. Write what you love about that person and how they make you feel.
4. Now put down your pen, close your eyes, and imagine what it feels like or felt like to be with that person. Allow a smile to come to your face if it arises.
5. Now check in with your body again. Write down the number on a scale of one to ten relating to the peace and joy you feel now.

    It's higher than the first number, isn't it? You just changed your frequency! Whether it moved one digit or made a huge jump, you changed your radio station. This is just the beginning of how you will reduce your anxiety and create the life you want.

# CHAPTER THIRTEEN

~

# Spidey Senses

"Would you like to try a piece of a gluten-free muffin?" A man called to me from behind his booth at my favorite farmer's market.

"Sure!" My arm stretched out for the tantalizing toothpick. "Mmm-mmm. So good." I felt bad about not buying his delectables, but I was pretty sure that was par for the course. Sort of like Costco but with fresh air and sunshine.

*I love Sunday mornings.* "Yes, please." I took a bite from one of my favorite grapes. I would swing back for those at the end. My routine involved making a couple of rounds, sampling my favorites, eating a tamale with goat cheese and green pepper, grabbing a latte, and then buying my usuals at the end, sparing my arm from lugging a heavy grocery bag.

For some reason, the fresh eggs drew me in. They were there every week, but to me they were usually irrelevant. But on this Sunday, I found myself pondering them and wanting to buy a carton.

*You should buy some,* the little voice inside me said.

Then my logical brain kicked in, *Why? You're working all week. You're never going to make yourself breakfast, it'll be a waste.* Since my brain is the smart one, I listened and continued on my merry way.

That night I got a call from my brother-in-law, "Hey, listen, I'm taking your sister to the hospital; can you come pick up the kids and keep them with you tonight?"

"What's wrong?" I said as my heart sank into my stomach.

"Not sure yet," he said. "She's having bad cramps. She thinks it her cyst thing."

Somewhat relieved, "I'm on my way." I jumped in my car, pajamas, and all.

It was bittersweet. Of course, I felt bad for my sister, but she had been through this before, and I knew she would be okay, but I *loved* having my niece and nephew sleep over. My niece, whom I refer to as my Soul Candy was five and my nephew, three, goes by my Angel of Love. I would distract them with cuddles and bedtime stories replete with silly voices for every character.

In the morning my niece crawled under the covers with me, and we giggled while my nephew slept like he had been drugged with an elephant tranquilizer. When he finally woke up we made our way downstairs.

"Aunt La, I'm hungry," he said.

"Okay, let's take a look," I made my way to the pantry. "How about some cereal?"

"No," he was blunt. "I want your magic ketchup eggs."

I called it magic because the mere addition of ketchup made the otherwise plain "gross eggs" not only delicious but sought-after.

"Yay! Magic ketchup eggs!" My niece bee-lined from my couch into the kitchen.

The little voice inside my head rebuked, *I told you to buy eggs, but you had to listen to "logic."*

*How did you know?* I thought.

*I'm your intuition. I know what's coming even when you don't. You really ought to start listening to me.*

*You're probably right.*

My logical self bristled. It was at that moment that I realized my intuition had a connection to the future that my brain didn't. Sometimes I ignored it, sometimes I listened, but I never thought of it as a true source of information. Boy, was I wrong.

## Anxiety User Manual: Intuition—Turning Up the Volume of the Little Voice Inside

Did you ever wonder how the world would be different if it weren't for intuition? Let's say you'd like to go to Rome. But would it be the Rome we know today if Julius Caesar had listened to his wife Calpurnia's sense that he should not go to the senate that night? On the subject of women's intuition, did you know that Ulysses S. Grant was supposed to attend the play at the Ford Theatre with Abraham Lincoln? But he stayed home and *did* listen to his wife's "gut feeling," only to find out that he, too, was an intended target for James Wilkes Booth.

Traveling to Europe might be different if in the 1950s Bill Allen, CEO of Boeing defense planes, ignored his sixth sense and listened to the people who called him crazy for thinking people would fly for fun. He put his money where his intuition was and spent $16 million to create the first 707 transcontinental commercial airplane.

Intuition was the basis for Ray Kroc's McDonald's drive-thru. He borrowed $2 million on a hunch that the smartest of businessmen scoffed at. It is known that more than 85 percent of top executives such as Richard Branson make decisions based on their gut feelings rather than data and analytics that disagree with their gut feelings.

Steve Jobs said, "Intuition is more powerful than intellect."

When anxiety is controlling your life, it can be very difficult to distinguish between fear and the little voice inside. So, how does one know the difference between your anxiety and your intuition? Why can fear be present as intuition? When we have had trauma in our past, our gut feelings can be conflated with our learned fear. For example, if Calpurnia had been married to a man before Julius Caesar who had been murdered, her prediction would have likely been attributed to a trauma trigger, not a premonition.

Anxiety feels different than intuition, even though they both are felt in our gut region, near our solar plexus chakra. Remember anxiety is a liar that predicts doom. If your stomach feels nervous and shaky you can tell it is a fear-based thought.

Intuition comes with a different feeling. With intuition there is a sense of excitement accompanied by a calm, inner knowing. It does not feel panic-like, but rather thrilling, steady, and true. It feels like a connection to source energy. The more you listen, the more you will build trust with that smart little voice. It propels you toward an action rather than causing you to shy away from it. It wants you to reach out, rather than pull in.

My intuition has helped me with many major life decisions. However, the most common communication from this sixth sense is about small, everyday moments, like the eggs. It will tell me to take my running shoes when I have no plans to run, but end up going for an unexpected walk with a friend after work. Or, to check my bank balance, only to find an incorrect charge, that I might have missed had I not looked at that precise moment.

While science is still limited, there are indications that time is relative to this dimension, meaning in some other dimensions, the events that we are experiencing now have already happened in these other dimensions. Einstein's math exposed the existence of the Big Bang Theory and black holes, but there was no way to prove its existence until science caught up with the math. Currently, the efficacy of the Big Bang Theory is in question. Today's math, according to some theoretical physicists like Brian Greene, has found information that indicates the existence of a multiverse.

Science may need to catch up to feel confident in this hypothesis. I don't. I, and many others that I know, access knowledge about future phenomena without knowing it, until it happens of course. This is my reason for listening to incoming information about events that have yet to enter my conscious awareness. That little voice inside has access to a different plane of my existence. It has the ability to acquire knowledge that is not otherwise available to me. I agree with what Albert Einstein said of intuition: "I believe in intuitions and inspirations . . . I sometimes *feel* that I am right. I do not *know* that I am." Intuition has foresight.

In hindsight, my intuition spoke to me my whole life, but it became more prolific when I felt connected to source energy, and I learned the difference between fear and gut feelings. We are getting information from the universe all the time through waves of energy and vibration. If something is giving you "good vibes" or "bad vibes" that's source energy communicating to you through your intuition.

The good news about intuition is that it helps you to build trust in yourself and trust in the universe. The more trust you have, the less anxiety you feel. If you know something bigger than yourself is caring for you, and you know how to hear and connect with it, then fear becomes irrelevant noise.

An acronym for "fear" that I like is False Evidence Appearing Real.

When you can distinguish between your anxiety and gut feelings, you will know the right answers and you will have the skills to separate the anxiety that is falsely predicting doom. Your Capable Adult Self will hear your intuition, listen to it, and soothe your anxiety-ridden Wounded Child.

## Build Your Toolkit

A simple way to check in with your intuition is the good old-fashioned coin flip.

Example: You get into two different colleges, UCLA and Ithaca. You're not sure which one you should pick. Make UCLA heads and Ithaca tails. Flip the coin. If you are disappointed with the side that came up it's the other one your intuition wants. If you like the results, you will feel relief or joy. You have been listening to or ignoring your gut feelings your whole life. It's important for you to build a sense of trust with your little voice inside.

Get your anxiety user manual.

1. Write down a time you can remember listening to your gut feeling. Write down how that feeling felt inside. Where did you feel it in your body, and what energy does it have as you are recalling now? Did it make you want to reach out and do it?
2. List a time you ignored your intuition.
3. Again, write down how it felt inside when you acted against your gut. Where did you feel it in your body and what energy did it have? Did I make you shut down inside, or withdraw?
4. Think about a decision you need to make today. It could be as small as what you want for dinner. Do you feel drawn to your answer and compelled to move forward? Or does it feel uncomfortable?
5. From now on, when that little voice of intuition pops into your head, whether it's a big decision or a seemingly insignificant one *listen to it!*

# CHAPTER FOURTEEN

~

# Thank You for Letting Me Be of Service

Until I got sober, I did not know that most churches and temples had additional rooms and that they rented space to twelve-step programs. No matter the size, they could all be described the same way. One corner is lined with empty racks, which moments before held folding chairs of either metal, plastic, or wood; whatever the material, all of them are uncomfortable. Someone from the AA meeting has taken a set-up commitment, and for one year, arrived early and arranged them in rows throughout the room. There is a plastic table against one wall, set up by the coffee commitment person, that has an urn of coffee, powdered creamer, sugar, and paper cups. Napkins, forks, and a cake, brought by the cake commitment person, are to be presented to anyone at the meeting celebrating one or more years of sobriety.

The beauty is that regardless of the location, size, or type of chair, these rooms are filled with community, laughter, and warmth for anyone who is seeking it. It is this kind of room helped me build my self-esteem when I was at an all-time low and continues to keep my spirits up regularly.

I could hear the sounds of merriment as the greeters met me at the door, welcoming me with a handshake, as they committed to do every week. Tonight is a speaker meeting, the opportunity to listen to a fellow

AA member share their experience, strength, and hope of their journey to and in sobriety.

The meeting began, and the secretary stood behind the podium addressing the meeting. "It is with great pleasure that I introduce to you our speaker for this evening, Laura Rhodes." My palms were a little sweaty, and my heartbeat quickened. I knew that was just my body gearing up to perform.

From the podium, "I'm Laura and I'm an alcoholic." The words left my mouth with joy, not shame.

The expected AA welcome dutifully echoed through the room. "Hi, Laura."

"If it's dry mouth you're looking for, you don't need to smoke pot, just stand in front of a crowd to speak, and voila," I say with candor.

The room laughs with me.

"I won't bore you with a drunkalogue, but trust me, I belong here. I'd rather focus on how the steps changed my life. Why, to me, they are the stairway to paradise and how they and of course, all of you taught me how to like myself."

The nods of identification drifted across the crowd.

"In steps one, two, and three you showed me that my way of navigating life's problems wasn't working and that there was a higher power that I could depend on that would guide me to make different choices. That was so hard to believe, and it was the last thing in the world I wanted, but it is the greatest gift I've ever been given." I giggle. "I can't believe I didn't think there was anything in the world more powerful than myself, or that I would resist having access to such an amazing force!"

The old-timers were amused, and the newcomers clenched up.

"Four, five, and six were real game changers. They helped me to understand why my self-esteem had sunk so low. But the best part about them was that they made it safe to figure out where I was going wrong. How my behavior was hurtful to myself and the people around me. Not just with the drinking, but those steps helped me find my part in every resentful situation throughout my life. Deconstructing my resentments led me to realize I could change my behaviors that were fueled by fear, and therefore, change the outcomes. I took everything personally, and my ego was very sensitive and let's just say, I'm a little controlling."

The audience chuckled.

"I was more worried about what you thought of me, than how I could help you. Seven, eight, and nine gave me the opportunity to right my wrongs. Not only did they repair the relationships I had with other people, but they also enabled me to repair the relationship I had with myself. I needed forgiveness from those I had harmed, and I needed forgiveness for the troubled thinking and behavior I had inflicted on myself. These steps revealed the patterns that were creating so many problems in my life.

"While those steps broke things down for me, it was ten, eleven, and twelve that built me back up. They taught me how to listen to my intuition, and how to trust myself. They showed me how to build my self-esteem. It may seem obvious now that giving fills me up, but I never knew how rich being of service to others was.

"I remember my sponsor saying, 'If you want to build your self-esteem, do esteem-able things.' Duh!"

I feign hitting myself on the forehead and the congregation laughs with me.

"I felt like a stranger when I first arrived in AA. You told me, 'Take a commitment.' You should always have one at your meetings, so I did, and it got me involved. It made me a part of the community. People thanked me for bringing the literature, or the cookies, taking out the trash —whatever my commitment, it connected me to the group. Newcomers, these acts may seem small and irrelevant, but it was by taking these actions that I slowly started to feel better about myself."

I made eye contact with a newcomer who still looked isolated and depressed and sent him warmth.

"These steps taught me the equation for happiness! I didn't understand that the core of connection and happiness was giving help to others and accepting help for myself. It was never put to me so simply."

I went on, "This is what I tell people about AA. How do you describe what chocolate tastes like to someone? You can say it's creamy, it's sweet, it's rich, but you can't reeeealllly describe the taste of chocolate. And if you hand it to someone, it kind of looks like a piece of shit. Shit with a bunch of nuts. Well, that's what Alcoholics Anonymous looked like to me. Shit with a bunch of nuts."

The group laughed.

"But it is the best, sweetest, and most delicious thing I've ever experienced. Thank you for making my cup run over. Thank you to every one of you who has a commitment, whether it is a designated position or the basic willingness to be here every week, sit in a chair, and make this a place where I can grow, learn, love you, and learn to love myself. Thank you for letting me be of service."

They applauded as I returned to my seat. What a night. So many more to come. I was high as a kite, and not from using, from sharing. No shame, no guilt, just self-love. From the bottom of my heart, thank you, Alcoholics Anonymous.

## Anxiety User Manual: The Fountain of You

I spoke in the last chapter about intuition. A big factor in helping me trust my intuition was to increase the trust I had in myself. By helping others, I learned how to help myself. Self-esteem is so important, and one of the best ways to build it is to give of yourself to others. It is a vital part of well-being.

I've learned that life is like a fountain. If you take and never give you become bloated and stagnant. If you give and never receive, you are running on empty. But if you learn how to give *and* receive, with *all of your might*, you will flow over with abundance.

Let's unpack that a little bit. "Takers" are labeled as selfish. With takers, it's all about them and their needs. The negative impact it has on those they deplete is irrelevant to them because they get their needs met. While these actions make them feel good in the short term, they do very little for self-esteem and self-respect.

Then there are the "people pleasers," those who give endlessly and never opt to receive. Some are tired, bitter, and feel underappreciated. "All I do is give, give give . . . and what do I get for it? Nothing." The quintessential martyr. Some are not resentful, just exhausted. The last person on their list to take care of is themselves. Their consciousness of deserving is low. They believe that receiving is selfish. Ironic, because that means that anyone they are giving to is by default selfish, even if they might not see it that way.

Then there are the "healthy" people. These are the people who are happy to give and help, but not at the expense of their own well-being. They know to put the proverbial oxygen masks on themselves first. They understand that giving feels good and that receiving is an opportunity to help someone else feel their value as well. The more they give, the more they are open to receiving. It is a flow. The consciousness of deserving is based on self-love.

Ego and self-love are opposites. To put it simply, ego, the part of us that comes from insecurity and lack is glad to take from others or do better than others. Whereas self-love seeks to nurture ourselves and those around us. It understands that we *all* need help and it's important to allow it and be grateful for it. The more love, compassion, and abundance there is in the world, the more beautiful and peaceful the world will become. So, love yourself! And love others! Be part of the solution, not the problem.

## Build Your Toolkit

Short-term ways to build your self-esteem by giving to others:

1. Return your shopping cart to the cart return. If you already do that, take an extra cart as well.
2. Return one call or email from your list every day.
3. Call someone out of the blue and thank them for something they did or give them a genuine compliment.
4. Do something nice for someone and don't tell anyone else about it. Just knowing inside can be enough, and it creates the opportunity for you to meet your needs without the recognition of others.
5. Let someone go in front of you in the grocery line.
6. Donate five dollars to a charity you feel is important.
7. Pick a flower and give it to someone you care about.

Long-term ways to build your self-esteem by giving to others:

1. Volunteer once a week, or once a month for a local establishment.
2. Do the weekly shopping for an older person you know.

3. Send monthly support to a child in a third-world country through a reputable organization.
4. Get in the habit of sending a card to someone you care about every month just because.
5. Once a month pay for a coffee for the person behind you in line.
6. Keep an old purse or bag in your car that has some essentials like gum, toothpaste, snack bars, tampons, or tissues and give the bag to a homeless person that you might pass by. When it's gone, make a new one.
7. Start a college savings account for a young person in your family and put in ten dollars a month.

# CHAPTER FIFTEEN

~

# Staying Inside Your Box

The smell of my coffee invited me to start the day, warming my throat as my eyes drifted to the sun shining over the mountains, and through my window on a beautiful Saturday morning. Putting my coffee cup on my bedside table, I stretched my arms, my back, and even my face as a stretching noise escaped through my mouth. *Life is good.*

I shuffled to my front door and grabbed the L.A. *Times* from the welcome mat. *Nice shot, newspaper boy.* I closed the door and headed back to the coffee and comfy sheets awaiting my return, lest they both cool down too quickly. As I settled in, the phone rang.

"Helloooo," I crooned into the receiver.

It was my aunt, who was far less relaxed than I was, "Hi, I'm going crazy!"

I sipped my coffee, "Do tell." I had already assumed the drama involved my mother, who lived in Vancouver but was staying at my aunt's house.

"It's my sister and your sister," she continued.

In my best W. C. Fields voice, I responded, "Ah, yesss."

"Your mother is too tired to drive over an hour to your sister's house. I told her to tell your sister it's too far, but when she gets on the phone with her, she acts like it's no big deal. But then she hangs up and complains that your sister wants her to drive all the way to her house. So, I say to her 'Why can't she come here?'"

"Makes sense," I responded.

She went on, "So, she says that your sister doesn't want to put the kids in the car for such a long drive, but they really want to see their grandmother. I want to call her and tell her to come here, but your mother won't let me."

"Okay, I get it." My mind started going through the scenarios of how to fix the situation.

She continued her desperation, "Would you call your sister, or talk some sense into your mother?"

My body began to leave its relaxed state to direct this drama in such a way that everyone would arrive at a happy ending. But in reality, it would've ended in one of two ways. An exhaustive, fruitless effort or a tension-filled fight between all parties. Then I caught myself. I paused. *Why do I have to get involved? I'm having such a lovely morning. Why does my aunt have to get dragged into this? Camp David, we were not.*

"Ya know . . . " I said.

"Yeah?" She inquired.

"This is not either of our problems. My sister is a grown woman, so is your sister. This is between the two of them. Let them figure it out. Why should we step in between two freight trains? I'm sure they will both survive either way, and without our quote-unquote help," I said, posing a new approach to family chaos.

She paused.

Then, "Oh, my God."

More silence, "You're right." She had seen the light.

"This is between them." She thought aloud, "Why should we get involved? It's not going to do any good anyway. You're right, they will both just get annoyed and frustrated with us."

"Yes!" We were both still surprised at the novelty being proposed.

Then I heard her laugh. "You're a genius. I'm going to have a bagel."

"Great idea! I will too," I laughed back.

"I love you," she said as she went to hang up.

"I love you too, bye," I said still giggling.

"Bye." She hung up.

I went back to my beautiful peaceful morning. Crisis averted. The coffee was a little cooler, but so was I.

## Anxiety User Manual: Setting Healthy Boundaries

I want to help you understand that setting boundaries does not make you a bad guy, it makes you a healthy guy. Unless you are a professional ambassador, stepping in and solving problems between two people you know or care about is not your job. Surprise! As noble as it may seem, it really isn't. In the field of psychology, this is referred to as "triangulation" and it is a poor way to communicate. Not only is it potentially problematic for you, but it is unhealthy for the relationships you are trying to fix, reinforcing that they are incapable of appropriate one-to-one communication. Let me explain why that is.

Triangulation is a passive-aggressive approach to problem-solving. It can also be manipulative, sometimes intentionally and sometimes not. The story I shared involved two different triangles. The first was my mother, trying to get my aunt to step in and fix the problem she was having with her own daughter. From her angle she wouldn't look like the bad guy, and also wouldn't have to make a long drive, but my aunt gets thrown under the bus in the process.

Then instead of my aunt setting a boundary with my mother and encouraging her to solve her own problem, my aunt called me to fix my sister, trying to spare herself the looming difficulty with either my sister, my mother, or both. In a time when I had fewer coping mechanisms, I would have jumped in to save the day. But whose day was I saving exactly? Someone was going to be unhappy, and my lovely morning could have flown right out of the window. A problem between two people should remain between two people.

Parents get the worst end of the triangulation stick. Children discover at an early age that they can get what they want from one parent, by going to the other and complaining. It is one of the most common disrupters of otherwise happy marriages, and the first place children learn coping skills that do not serve them in the long run.

Perhaps you're thinking, *What if I can solve the problem and make both people happy?* I hate to break it to you, but it is still dysfunctional.

People need to learn how to express their needs and get them met through direct communication. Mommy isn't going to call your boss, or your friends, or your partner and fix your problems. You have to learn how to do that all on your own. If not, you learn that triangulation is an effective way to get your needs met.

It is a bad approach for the person starting the triangle. Taking the easy way out and having someone else do the dirty work is an unhealthy and selfish way to resolve your problems, even if it is not meant with bad intentions.

It is also a predicament for the person being triangulated. They have been put in the middle, and should they opt to help, they are empowering poor relationship skills. Most people don't even know they are doing anything wrong. They step on board the drama train, in a valiant effort to be the "super fixer" and in doing so surrender their own serenity.

The best way to learn how to set boundaries is to imagine you are standing inside a hula hoop. That is the size of *your* box. Anything that happens outside of your box is in *someone else's* box. This might be a shocker but nothing outside of your box is your business. In addition, no one gets to come inside your box and tell you how to handle your life or the choices you make. That does not mean every choice you make has to be the right choice. Wrong choices help us learn too. Your Capable Adult Self knows that.

Inside your box there is only room for two people, at best. So, if you have a problem, and you'd like help, you can invite someone inside your box and get their advice. Once that is done, you don't send that advice giver into someone's box to solve your problem. They go back to their own box. Then, you invite the person you have the problem with into your box and fix the issue between the two of you.

If someone has an interpersonal problem, they would like your help in addressing, they can ask you for advice about how to step into someone else's box, which you do or do not have to give them. That is your choice. But you don't go and pull a third person into the box and tell them how to handle the issue they are having with the other person. There is not enough room for three people in the box. It is crowded and inappropriate at its best, and cramped and combative at worst. Stay inside your own box.

This also applies to watching two people in someone else's box. You don't get to run over and insert yourself because you think you know best. You stay inside your box, mind your own business, and let them learn how to problem solve. They may not get it right, but it is their lesson to figure it out.

You certainly don't go over to someone else's box, let yourself in, and tell them they are doing something incorrectly. No matter how good our intentions might be, you do not have the right to tell people how to live their lives, and the good news here is that no one gets to tell you how to live yours.

Last but not least, if your counsel has been requested, and you have been invited into another's box you may step in, or you can choose not to. That is up to you. No one comes into your box unless you want them there, and you don't have to go into anyone else's unless you'd like to.

I'd like to make it clear that "no" is a complete sentence. You do not have to explain to anyone why you don't want to do something or why you do not wish to get involved. You can, but you do not have to. To most people the why doesn't matter, it's just another avenue to find their way to a yes.

Learning how to set your boundaries will make your life a lot more peaceful and will put a big dent in your issues with anxiety.

## Build Your Toolkit

Get your user manual. Let's identify your triangles.

1. Are you the middle person or mediator in some of your relationships? Yes, or no?
2. Do you see that as a common role you play in life? Yes, or no?
3. If the answer was yes to either question, does it give you anxiety when you do it? Yes, or no? If the answer is yes, give yourself permission to turn in your ambassador hat. If your answer is no, and it gives you a feeling of accomplishment, remember that you might be enabling dysfunctional communications for people you care about.

4. If a plain no is hard to say at first, here are some other ways to kindly set your boundaries.

"Now is not a good time."

"I have too much on my plate right now."

"I don't want to bite off more than I can chew."

"The two of you need to figure this one out on your own."

"I am not comfortable getting involved with this."

5. Are you a person who has trouble approaching others, and therefore asks others to step in? Yes, or no?

6. If the answer is yes, write down the fear that causes you to seek others to mitigate your issues.

If you see approaching others as confrontational, I have written the next chapter just for you. If you don't, you have the opportunity to learn some new ways to approach your relationships.

# CHAPTER SIXTEEN

~

# I Need . . .

It was Valentine's Day 2018. My husband and I agreed that we wouldn't exchange gifts this year. This was a commercial Hallmark holiday that was accompanied by overly expensive flowers and dinners, not a necessary occasion to express our love. We knew we loved each other and a regular night at home was sensible and easy.

I stopped at the market to grab some lunch on my way to work. The heart-shaped balloons festooned the entrance, and the perfumed lilies intoxicated me. So much for being sensible. *I should get some flowers for the people at the office. They are so dedicated. It would be nice, and they would appreciate it, especially those who might feel a little alone today.* Holidays tend to do that. They either fill people with joy and love or can be a cruel highlight of loneliness. I picked individual roses in different colors that reflected each person's personality. It felt good handing them out when I got to work, and I wasn't the only one who was struck by Cupid's spirit. Other people had left candies in little red totes or small tokens for each other to be found when we got into our offices.

Out of nowhere a pang of emptiness reached into my stomach. I checked in with myself. *What's that about?* I was surprised and disappointed with the answer. I wanted a present or at least something from my husband. *Are you really going to be one of those women who needs a material gift? You have a great marriage. This is so childish.* I dismissed the feeling and went on with my day. But the cloying yen of wanting was stuck there.

I should share that my mother's love language was gift-giving. There wasn't a holiday that went by that didn't involve lavish exchanges of love. My mother was delighted to get presents and she was generous in giving them. For example, on my sixteenth birthday, I was awakened by my high school's marching band coming through my bedroom door accompanied by all my friends yelling "Surprise!" Suffice it to say, I had grown accustomed to elaborate exchanges on special days. *No pressure, future boyfriends.* Even though my Capable Adult Self knew that my husband loved me and that I didn't need a material token to know he did, my Wounded Child had learned that love came gift-wrapped, and she felt sad without one. So, the two of me needed to have a conversation.

Wounded Child: "I really want a present."

Capable Adult Self: "That's what you learned growing up."

Wounded Child: "I know he loves me, it makes no sense, and if I ask now, I'll seem needy and insecure."

Capable Adult Self: "Judging yourself much? It sounds to me like you would be expressing an emotional need. Emotions and logic are different entities."

Wounded Child: "I don't want to make him feel bad. We already agreed."

Capable Adult Self: "But *you* feel bad right now. That is definitely not what he'd want. He loves you; he'll understand."

I called my husband.

"I need a tchotchke. I know we agreed not to get anything each other, but would you mind? I feel silly asking, but for some reason, I need it." I was surprised to feel a lump in my throat.

He chuckled. "You crack me up. I'm on it! The ignoring Valentine's Day plan felt a little weird for me too. I love it when you get me cards."

The lump in my throat dissolved into a smile. "I love you so much. You're the best."

"Love you too, Sweetie. See you later," he said as we hung up.

*He does love cards. I'll find a romantic one and a funny. Win, win.*

The pit in my stomach disappeared as peace flowed in. I had expressed my need and my husband was prepared to meet it. Our friends and family are not mind readers. Sometimes they know what we want without us having to ask, but sometimes they don't. In this case, I didn't even know that I would like a Valentine's present until I felt it inside. I could have dismissed the thought. I could have shamed myself and left it at that. But I have learned to listen to my emotions and express them in a healthy way. Stating my needs is vital to my well-being. When my relationships have true intimacy, I am safe to express my needs.

## Anxiety User Manual: Confrontation, Expression, and Imtimacy

Many people are afraid to express their needs based on the misconception that it is confrontation. Even something as small as asking the server at the restaurant to have the chef cook your steak more to your liking can feel like confrontation. But it is not. It is expressing your desire to have the steak you are paying for made the way you like to eat it.

Is the person dining worried about not being liked or causing trouble for the kitchen, or maybe their mother always made a scene at restaurant, so now a simple request feels unseemly or rude? The chef or server might indeed be annoyed, but they might not be. The point is it doesn't matter. It's not that I don't care about how the chef or server feels, it's that sometimes getting your needs met is not what someone else wants, but that doesn't mean you shouldn't have your needs met.

Your Wounded Child will be the one fretting about upsetting the chef, but since we know that always underneath anger is fear, then, if the chef is angry, it is his Wounded Child reacting because he is either insecure or just really busy. But his Capable Adult Self knows it is his job to prepare the meal to your liking, and your Capable Adult Self will know that it's okay to ask for your steak to be cooked properly.

This may be a trivial example, but life is full of happenings both trivial and important in which asking for what you need can become a source of anxiety or depression. Why should you have anxiety about enjoying life to its fullest? What brings us discomfort when we are asking to have our needs met? This is part of learning how to love yourself. Love yourself enough to meet your own needs and get them met by others. If you are looking out for the chef and the chef is looking out for the chef, who is looking out for you? No one. It is natural and healthy to look out for yourself.

What I am talking about is *intimacy*.

My definition of intimacy: Emotional safety is the ability to be emotionally naked with someone and feel safe. Whether the other person agrees or not there is no judgment or defensive response, only a willingness to listen and let the other person be heard.

However, to have intimacy with others you must first have intimacy with yourself. It is normal and healthy to have needs, and we shouldn't prioritize how others might judge our needs over getting our needs met.

When I meet with two people who are having issues—that is, couples or parents and teens—they often share with me that they have communication problems. My response is as follows. I tell one of them to ask the other to pass them a tissue. As expected, it is executed, and within seconds one has passed the other a Kleenex. They have no trouble communicating. What they are struggling with is the ability to feel safe when it comes to expressing their emotions. They do not have intimacy. They fear that expressing their needs will be met with rejection and or judgment. They misinterpret expression as confrontation and therefore are not able to simultaneously state their need and feel safe doing it. Instead, they repress their needs and resent each other. Or they let the resentment build and finally scream their needs through the voice of Wounded Child, instead of clearly expressing what they want with Capable Adult Self, and the results do not end well.

There is a great expression, "Say what you mean, mean what you say, and don't say it mean."

Confrontation is a potentially heated exchange between two people who are at odds with each other.

Expression is a desire to share your feelings with another and achieve understanding.

These two concepts get confused.

Learning to express your needs enables you to create the life you want to live. When you discard your needs, you will find yourself surrounded by people who continue to discard your needs. By having a healthy relationship with yourself, you will naturally attract good relationships in life. The stability and respect in your relationships are a direct reflection of the connection and love you have for yourself.

If you demand a good work environment, you will find one, or it will find you. If you feel deserving of loving relationships, you will create them. If you allow people to discard your needs and walk all over you, sadly, they will. When we neglect our needs, our anxiety lets us know, by making us very uncomfortable. We can thank our anxiety for being such a caring alert system.

If I neglect my needs, I am bitter and resentful of the people around me and they respond in kind. If I hate my meal, I will not return to that restaurant. If I resent my husband my relationship is miserable. If I neglect my employees, my business will suffer. When we walk on eggshells, nothing breaks, but no one has breakfast either.

Conversely, if I take care of my wants and desires, I feel inner peace and happiness, and so do the people around me. It makes the chef feel good when I thank him for going the extra mile. It made my husband happy to get me a gift. It makes me happy when my employees feel valued. Everybody wins!

I discussed in an earlier chapter that it feels good to give. I used to worry that asking for my needs to be met was putting someone else out. In *healthy* relationships, it is the opposite. It is giving a chance for someone that you love to feel valued and helpful. Giving feels good, and often in our misguided view of being needy, we deprive those around us of the opportunity to feel needed themselves. We all need to be needed, just as much as we want to be taken care of. If no one is asking to be helped, then no one gets the chance to be helpful. Love yourself and let the people around know how to do the same.

## Build Your Toolkit

Get your user manual.

1. Make a list of your needs that are not being met. Ask yourself, where do my relationships or life circumstances leave me wanting? Where do my expectations fall short of reality and end up disappointing me?
2. Now look at each item on your list. Have you asked for these needs to met *directly*?

3. If you have asked, did you ask with the voice of your Wounded Child, coming from a fearful or agitated state? Or the voice of Capable Adult Self, the calm clear self that can articulate without being accusatory?
4. If you have not asked for that need to be met, what is it that you are fearing? Rejection? Judgment?
5. Do you feel deserving of what you are asking for or do you feel self-judgment or low self-esteem?
6. Are you treating yourself with love and respect?
7. Write down three things you can do to meet your own needs.
8. In the voice of Capable Adult Self, write down three things you can ask someone else to do for you.

# CHAPTER SEVENTEEN

~

# Look for the Beauty

Despite the chaos from the night before, today's itinerary looked promising and full of fun. I would drive my sister, her husband, along with my niece and nephew to pick up the car they couldn't find the night before in the crowds of the Vancouver fireworks show. They had disagreed about where it was parked and were about to miss the last ferry back to the small island where my mother lived. They decided to leave the car and pick it up on the way to the next day's activities. The morning would start with breakfast on the water, then a visit to the Capilano Suspension Bridge, and end with a miniature train ride through Stanley Park. The kids were little, but they would love it and the joy of watching their smiling faces awaited us.

Since driving without car seats was not an option, we searched through the parking structure for half an hour, on foot until we located their lost rental.

"Oh, thank God!" my sister screeched.

A barrage of "yays" were echoed by the rest of us.

"Open the door, baby, these bags are heavy," she said to my brother-in-law.

"You have the keys, not me," he said.

"No, I don't. They were on the dresser by your wallet," her voice elevated with panic.

His voice heightened in anger, "I told you to grab them when I was going down the stairs."

This conversation did not unfold well, and the screaming family was now riding with me in my car, as I drove us all to breakfast in my rented Prius. As the thoughts in my head were bombarded with the crying and the yelling, my anxiety pushed its way to the surface and left me disconnected from anything besides the hysteria that reverberated through the tiny car. My Wounded Child squirmed with discomfort. My heart pounded harder, I held my breath, and my sweaty palms gripped the wheel. Then I heard Capable Adult Self trying to get my attention.

*Practice what you preach. Don't focus on the noise. This is their problem, not yours. You can still enjoy your day. What else is around you?* I felt my back relax, as a bald eagle in the distance caught my eye. The majesty of the mountains that surrounded me appeared like magic from the mist of the hysteria. I hadn't seen them on a conscious level until this moment. *What else is happening in this moment? I've never driven a Prius before this trip.* I trained my attention on the sounds emitted by the electric vehicle. I rolled down the window and breathed in the fresh air. The more I focused on what was in front of me and on the pleasant sensations that were available when I looked for them, the more the clamoring argument faded into the back seat where it belonged. Until I was able to draw my senses to the rest of the environment, it seemed like the fighting surrounded me, but now it didn't. There was so much more to experience. It's natural to pay attention to the loudest thing in the room, but with the right emotional tools, I chose a better experience for myself. The loudest moment isn't always the only one to focus on.

## Anxiety User Manual: True Peace Is Learning What to Ignore

What you choose to focus on in life is up to you. If you opt to pay attention to the chaos around you, your anxiety will engage, and your peace and serenity will fall away. But, if you teach yourself to concentrate on the good, the purposeful, the beauty of the moment, it is your anxiety that will slip into the background. I'm not saying you should ignore the problems in your life, but I am suggesting that every problem that is happening around you is not yours to embody. Or at least it doesn't have to be if you choose otherwise.

I've recently heard the phrase, "Not my circus, not my monkey," echoing through the zeitgeist. But the question remains, How does one leave the circus? Especially, when the cast of monkeys are your family, your friends, or your work environment. It's not to say that any one of those people is bad, it's that life can feel like a circus if you let it. I have shared the importance of staying inside your box, but if the boxes around you are loud and combative, how do you maintain peace and joy on your own? It is an acquired skill that takes self-love and practice.

When you are watching a sports event, do you ever wonder how the players are able to concentrate with all the screaming fans around them, booing or cheering? They do it with the laser focus they have practiced from the time they were in little league. I'm sure those ball players use the cheering to buoy their spirits, when necessary, but they do their darnedest to mute the booing because it does not serve their success.

Happiness takes work and the squeaky wheel doesn't always have to get the grease. It is your right to select what you will engage with from the variety of experiences available to you at any given moment. Take what you want and leave the rest.

Your Capable Adult Self and your senses are there to assist you in living the life you want. They are your conduits to the alternate, less obvious connections. I coach my patients who are approaching holiday times with dread to seek out the little things that can make moments pleasant. Even if it's as simple as noticing how lovely the cranberry sauce looks in that dish, and imagining the time and care it took to prepare it can cultivate peace inside. A tiny shift of focus can remove them from suffering through an ugly conversation at the table. Of course, people can choose to become involved in the debate unfolding in front of them, but they don't have to. They have alternatives.

We all have the option to tune in to what we want to when we have learned how. I listen to books on tape when I am in the dentist's chair. If you are stuck in traffic you can rage against the machine, you can listen to music, or call a friend, anything that will keep you company on the way. Frustration with the cars around you won't get you there any faster. But you might learn something interesting from a podcast if that's what you opt to do with that moment. Focusing on the unrelenting traffic will only spike your anxiety.

The truth is we are in control of very little. We are subject to weather, family, politics, communities, the list goes on ad infinitum. It is often our desire to be in control of that which we cannot affect, that contributes to our anxiety. We can fight the unresolvable or find peace by redirecting our attention to more fruitful events.

When we become adept with our emotional tools, we can separate from the unpleasant and unite with contentment. Oddly, it is when faced with extreme adversity that most of us realize this. It is the person with a fatal disease that appreciates the moment the most. Why should we have to come to such extreme measures to indulge ourselves in the little joys of life? Life is more about the little things than the big ones. The big ones are few and far between and are often accompanied by disappointment due to unrealistic expectations. There is so much pleasure to be found in the minutia. We are told not to sweat the small stuff but lack the insight to enjoy the tiny miracles happening around us all the time when we remember to look for them.

Life has plenty of unavoidable difficulties. So, it's important to learn how to skirt the unnecessary unpleasantries life's buffet can offer up and indulge in the good ones!

## Build Your Toolkit

For this toolkit I am going to walk you through an exercise. Complete each step without looking at the next step until it's time.

1. Find a large object in the room to focus on.
2. Describe the object aloud. Be thorough. What colors are in it? What does it feel like? What is its function? Does it have a temperature?
3. Now continue looking at the object but *do not* think about it. Did you find number three to be difficult?
4. Now turn your head away from the object and focus on a different large object.

5. Once again, describe the object aloud. Color, feel, purpose, and so on. You are no longer thinking about object number one, are you? You must change your focus to shift your experience.

Now get your user manual.

1. Write down in detail the last unpleasant experience you had. Write about the five senses, all of them, you can remember experiencing as you tell the story.
2. Now reflect on a different focal point you could have had during that same moment, again, using all your five senses.
3. Write about as many different experiences that might have been available in that moment for you to connect with. This will help you to switch moments in the future.

# CHAPTER EIGHTEEN

~

# Bad News

"This is the end of democracy as we know it!" screamed Chuck Schumer from the Senate floor.

"It's true," I heard myself say aloud. *It must be. You can say, "grab them by the pussy" and the conservative, church-going party will still vote for you? Laura! You know Donald Trump is a troubled man. The Republicans are not bad people! They are just afraid of different things than the Democrats. Everyone seems angry with everyone. Always under anger is fear! You are a therapist, don't give in to the hate.*

The news was my life. I watched it all morning before work, then I got home at night and watched every bit I missed. Most of it was redundant, but I had to keep abreast of current events. I would not be a sheep. I was determined to stay involved. My email flooded with urgent letters from Nancy Pelosi begging, "Send money now!" I did. Even though I lived in California, I sent money to Beto O'Rourke in Texas.

I tuned to Fox News to ensure I was getting both sides of the story.

"The Democrats want our guns. They always have. We must defend the Constitution!" a pundit professed.

"That's not true!" I yelled at the screen, again. "We just don't want people to buy AR-15s without proving they aren't crazy and about to blow down a school full of children, you fucking moron!" I fell back onto the couch in a sweat.

It was an entirely different story on liberal news channels. We all watched the news, and we believed what we heard. I believed what Rachel Maddow said and I'm sure conservatives believed Sean Hannity. *I feel sick to my stomach!*

I watched every vote that took place on the Senate floor. "Senator Grassley?"

Senator Grassley pressed his mic on, "Aye." He turned his mic back off.

"Senator Feinstein?" droned the moderator.

She flipped on her mic, "No."

I found myself watching reruns of the Senate floor specials from the nineties.

"This is the end of democracy as we know it!"

The Senate floor in the eighties.

"This is the end of democracy as we know it!"

The seventies.

"This is the end of democracy as we know it!"

The sixties.

"This is the end of democracy as we know it!"

Then it hit me. *I AM a sheep. I'm doing exactly what every smart person in America is doing. I listen to the politicians; I get scared and send them money.*

I continued deep in thought . . . *politicians have never created change! Change is produced by the people who are at the forefront of current movements. It is only enacted into law when people get so loud that politicians have to follow suit. They are overpaid pedantic puppets. All they care about is getting our money to keep their jobs. They scare us into believing we need their support. Change is not made through hate. Hate keeps us divided. The news and politicians keep telling us to hate each other, and we believe them!*

I turned off my television, deleted the myriad news recordings from my DVR, and flushed my proverbial sheep outfit down the toilet.

Then I had a lively conversation with myself.

"I am tired of feeling sick." I rubbed my stomach.

"Do I sit back and do nothing? That's not helpful." I resisted.

I sought my solution. *You can help in different ways, in your ways. You treat members from every political party at the center, and you love them all.*

*Their politics are irrelevant. Your job is to help them believe there is love and safety in the world, and how not to operate from fear and anger.*

"That's true," I responded aloud to my Capable Adult Self.

I started sending my money to the causes I believed in and not politicians. I do my best to focus my patients on health and well-being, not hate and fear-fueled anger. Life's too short, and so am I. I want to feel good inside. This plan works for me, and it works for my anxiety.

## Anxiety User Manual: Bring Peace to Yourself, and You Will Bring Peace to the World

Resentment is poison and has never helped anyone. The news media and politicians present the toxic side of issues and omit the heart-centered, authentic concerns, regardless of the party. Actions speak louder than words. The political climate does not seek to reach across the aisle. It leans toward black-and-white thinking, over-exaggeration, and divisive rhetoric. They tout that people are eating babies or seeking to arm criminal lunatics. They breed resentment and anger. Who does that help? It helps the lobbyists and the commercial advertisers. All the years of research connecting lung cancer and tobacco forced the hand of the lobbyists to put a mere label on cigarette packs. But politicians and the media don't care about our health, though they sure make a lot of money inundating us with ads that push every drug imaginable to their viewers.

Big pharma is one of the largest lobbyists in this country. They want us to be anxious. They want to mask symptoms rather than cure them. Curing the underlying disease teaches a person to fish, but they would rather have us mask the symptoms and buy the proverbial fish du jour from them at outrageous prices.

Watching the news along with the commercials that support it creates anxiety. They preach that the world and the people who live in it are unsafe. So, I don't watch the news anymore. You don't have to watch the news either if it is contributing to your anxiety. That doesn't mean that you don't care about current events, it just relieves you from bearing witness to fear-filled hyperbole. The media repeats the same problems over and over again. There is rarely anything new. Anything big enough and new enough you will end up hearing about without subjecting your nervous system to daily doses of fear.

I encourage you to save your energy for the solutions, rather than the problems. You know in your heart what is right and what is wrong for you. You don't need the media to tell you how to feel and who to fear. Love thy neighbor. You can find ways to be a positive contributor to the human race without all of that rhetoric. You can add to the betterment of humanity in your own ways. The beautiful thing is *that we each have different gifts to offer the world*. The planet needs each and *every* one of us to take care of issues that are important to us. *Vive la difference*.

Maybe you don't like litter, and you pick up pieces of plastic that you see on the street. Perhaps, being a part of your community church gives you joy, and that is how you help your fellow humans. Big gestures and small gestures can each make to help the planet be the kind of place we want to live in. In doing so, you begin to feel useful, empowered, and relevant. Most importantly, it will bring you peace, not anxiety.

In earlier chapters I discuss the vital nature of giving in regard to our mental health and self-esteem. This concept takes that kernel and applies it to the world in a bigger way. Watching the news and hating others does nothing to help you or the universe, it only nurtures anxiety. You reserve the right to do your part in creating harmony in the world, big or small. Send hope and good thoughts through the energy waves. Gandhi is credited with the phrase "Be the change you want to see in the world." Whether he said it or not, I believe it is true. This begs the question, Is hate what you want to see? I doubt it. Rid yourself of anxiety by focusing on peace and caring for what you believe in. If your brain is fed a steady diet of negativity, you will feel anxious and depressed. It follows then, that if you feed your brain positive information, you will feel happy, motivated, and serene. You can control what you watch on your television, what you read, and what populates your screens more than you realize. Whatever you put into your computer is what comes back.

Take this opportunity to assess your daily diet of the information you are consuming. What you ingest mentally predicts what you feel physically.

## Build Your Toolkit

Take an inventory of what you let into your world via television, your computer, your social media, and complete a thirty-day challenge.

1. Write a small entry in your user manual about how the current daily dose of information you absorb affects your anxiety.
2. Select the programs that contribute to your anxiety. I challenge you to change them for the next thirty days and watch shows that only help you to laugh and feel good, and do not provoke any anxiety.
3. I would like you to erase the search history on your computer. Now open a new tab and type in a topic that will bring you joy or positive thoughts. An item that piques your interest that you would like to learn more about. Now, open eighteen more tabs and do the same thing.
4. Turn on your social media outlets. Snooze the groups that bring you anxiety for thirty days. Search for groups that would promote positive interests for yourself and join them.
5. Set an alarm on your calendar for thirty days from now.
6. When the thirty days are over, go back to your user manual.
7. Write a small entry about how your anxiety has changed since the switch on your media resources.
8. Has your daily anxiety changed? Is it for the better? If the answer is yes, keep it that way.

# CHAPTER NINETEEN

~

# I Can't Make It through This

My father was dying. *I don't know how to do this.* I could hear it over and over. This phrase repeated in my head; it came out of my mouth, "I don't know how to do this." I tucked the lock of hair that fell into my mouth behind my ear, and it stuck to tears streaming down my face. He was one of my best friends in the whole world. My number one cheerleader.

I remembered pulling up to his car in a hospital parking lot two years ago on a trip we'd made *yet again* to help my grandmother. He looked at me and said, "Does it get any better than us?"

I said, "Impossible."

We both grinned from ear to ear as we drove off in separate directions.

*Dad can't be dying. It's always us in the hospital waiting room together. Not me out here alone.*

Now here I was, at the hospital, my grandmother was alive, well, and watching *The Price Is Right* in her apartment in Encino, and he was dying. MY father was in the next room, dying.

"I don't know how to do this," I say aloud again.

Capable Adult Self hugged me tightly. *But you are doing it. You're going to be okay. Death happens. It is normal to lose a parent. Dad will not be dying forever.*

Wounded Child burst through. *But he will be gone!*

Capable Adult Self answered. *Yes, but THIS pain, this unbearable torture, will fade with time. You only have to do this part once.*

Wounded Child grabbed the wheel. *We have done everything together. He can't die! If I ever needed him, he was there, no matter what. This isn't fair!*

Then my father's voice chimed into my inner dialogue, "Life isn't necessarily fair, Blacky."

Wounded Child screamed back! *This isn't life. This is death!*

Capable Adult Self sat down to face Wounded Child. *Do you expect him to walk you through his own death?* I searched for the tear-ravaged tissue in my jacket pocket to wipe my tears.

The last few weeks, as he lay in his hospital bed, he waxed philosophical and shared with me the epiphanies he was having about life, love, money, and the futility of chasing riches. At one point he motioned to the mezuzah that had hung around his neck since his twenties.

"Take this off of me and keep it with you when I die," he said, matter-of-factly.

I flashed back to my childhood when I had spent countless weekend mornings waiting for him to wake up so I could invade the king-size bed and cuddle with him while he read the paper. Laying on his chest, the smell of sleep lingered while I peered at the comic section over the mezuzah nestled in his chest hair.

Now he was in a hospital bed, and there was no room for me. I couldn't believe we were having these conversations. It's the one regret I have in my life. I couldn't walk him through this. He needed me to acknowledge that he was dying, and I couldn't. I waved off any discussions of his actual departure, denying him his truth. I held his hand, but I would not cross the threshold of a path that ended with his death. I tried to lead him down paths lined with false hopes.

I'd like to think my Capable Adult Self was in charge. But it wasn't.

I woke up with a start at 4:03 every morning for ten days before he died, and then my Wounded Child would pray, "Pleeeeeeeease save him!"

Then finally, when the end was imminent, and there was no choice but acceptance, I laid on his chest and cried to him for the last time, "Okay, Daddy. You can go." He needed to hear it. There was nothing else I needed to say. We had already said it all; I just had to say the words I couldn't utter until that moment.

That night I was startled awake by the phone ringing. "Is this Ms. Rhodes?

"Yes," I replied.

"Mr. Michael Rhodes has passed."

I was numb. My head was ringing. I looked across the room. The clock read 4:03. I keep his mezuzah next to my bed.

## Anxiety User Manual: This Too Shall Pass

This was the hardest moment of my life to date. I would rather have ten heart attacks than go through that again. However, while I miss him terribly, and long for his presence, sometimes more often than other times, the pain of his actual death, eventually passed. It took years, but it passed. The nightmares stopped, bursting into tears out of nowhere ceased, and I am a very happy person.

When I am facing hardships, this is the one phrase that helps me knuckle down, grit my teeth, and bear it. "This too shall pass." Every painful experience in life passes.

As human beings, we face so many pains and adversities in life. Financial fear can push anxiety to the brink. Heartbreak is another experience that can seem never-ending. But it does end. We go on to love another day eventually.

When anxiety hits, it may feel like that moment will never end. It may lead to dark thoughts like suicide so that the angst will finally stop. But you should *never* make a permanent choice over a temporary situation. Anxiety will always pass. Depression will pass. Trauma will pass, and sometimes just the simple knowing that you will feel different, eventually, will get you through anything.

*This too shall pass.* I encourage you to invite this helpful sentence into your inner dialogue. It is a tool that will buoy you through any storm.

When you find yourself feeling that you cannot stand even one more second of your anxiety or whatever it is that is troubling you "this too shall pass" is there for you. When it seems like you are alone and nothing and no one can help you, "this too shall pass" will. You might be wondering, *what is it about this four-word phrase that offers a guaranteed lifesaver when I am drowning?*

First, "this" can be anything. It can be a feeling, an event, a day, a moment, a death, an operation, a meeting with your boss, divorcing a spouse, a splinter in your finger, a car accident, food poisoning, a migraine, a panic attack. "This" can be anything.

Second, "too" reminds you of the resilience you have built in your life. In reflection, your life has already endured countless difficult events. Even if you don't remember it, you learned how to walk, to speak a language, to fall and get up, to cry and soothe yourself, you have already survived so much. "Too" lets us know that we have done hard things before and survived, and we can this time "too."

Third, "shall" gives us a tether to the future. It indicates that while *right now* it is painful, in the future it will be different. This is only for now. It "shall" be better in time. It is a word that guarantees a different time "shall" arrive.

And lastly, "pass." One day, in the near or distant future, this event will be over. You will no longer be experiencing it. It will not only have an end, but it will also be behind us, and this information is a valuable tool that helps you navigate the storm. There will be a chance to let go and breathe and be free of whatever anxiety, trouble, or issue you are having in that awful moment, no matter what. This storm, as every storm does, will "pass."

## Build Your Toolkit

Get your user manual.

1. Write the first time you can remember thinking, *I will never get through this.*
2. Then write down how you did it.
3. Write down how long it took.
4. Now write down the hardest thing you have ever done.
5. Then write how you did it.
6. Write down how long it took.

7. Write down the next thing in your life that is coming that you are having anxiety about it.
8. Now write down how you will get through it.
9. Is there an alternate, more ideal way you'd like to get through number 7?
10. Write down the ideal way to get through number 7.
11. Now visualize it happening the way you want and remind yourself that no matter how it unfolds . . . this too shall pass.

# CHAPTER TWENTY

~

# Her Pain Is Awful

It had been a tense week. Work ran me ragged; My husband and I had barely spoken. We weren't fighting, but we were ships passing in the night. I thanked God it was Saturday, and we had the weekend to relax, enjoy, and hang out. Then the phone rang.

I glanced at the caller ID: TGOLDBERG.

*That's weird. She never calls me.* I hadn't spoken to this woman in almost six months. Soon after losing my father, I rented her guest house for a year, and at that time, we were close.

She was as grounded and graceful as the trees shading her beautiful property, and I never once saw anything bother her. We got married in her backyard a few years after I moved out.

"Hello!" I answered with joy. Joy is not what I heard on the other end. I heard a sob. She cried her nickname for me in her Israeli accent, "Laurcheh?"

"What's wrong?" I said.

"It's my daughter. I am at UCLA."

"What happened?" My voice reflected her worry.

"She's dying, Laurcheh. Kencer. It's in her lungs and everywhere."

We spent the next hour and a half on the phone. I looked at my husband on the couch, knowing he would be bummed at hearing my next question to her.

"Do you want me to come to UCLA?"

He waved his hand, indicating he got it, and relieved me of any guilt for going to the hospital if she needed me.

"No. Vee don't want anyone. I just needed to hear your voice. Send prayers, Laurcheh. Send light. Every bit helps."

"Absolutely." I was already closing my eyes to send healing energy. We expressed love to each other and hung up.

*Well, I guess we will not relax and enjoy the day. How can we do that knowing what that family is going through?* I knew firsthand the rapacious nature cancer had on families. My body and heart hung heavy with sadness.

The voice of my Capable Adult Self whispered to me from inside. *You're not a bad person if you still enjoy the day with your husband.*

The ears of my Wounded Child perked up like a puppy, hearing a chance to go for a walk.

Capable Adult continued. *You love her, and she knows it. You spent half the morning supporting her as you should, but you having a miserable day isn't going to help her or her daughter. You need a day to refill your tank. You and your husband need to reconnect this weekend.*

Wounded Child and Capable Adult went back and forth until Capable Adult won the day. Weight poured off my shoulders. I went to my husband on the couch.

"You okay, Baby?" he said.

"You know what? Thank God I am. Let's pray for them and then go enjoy our weekend." The liberation was palpable. We sent love and light their way and then we refilled our emotional tanks with a wonderful day of golf and a sunset dinner at the beach.

## Anxiety User Manual: You Don't Need to Feel Everyone's Pain to Be a Good Person

I remember *choosing* not to feel sadness. It was the first time I had made a conscious decision not to feel guilty that I wasn't embodying the pain of others. The act of carrying the hurt for others, friends, family, and the world has been a part of me ever since I can remember. My worry had never helped anyone. But it had stolen a plethora of peace and serenity from me, time and time again.

My care, on the other hand, has helped many. I will always care. I will always do anything within my power to help those I love. But suffering with them is futile. Suffering for others is anxiety-provoking, draining and unproductive.

When something goes wrong in the world, I hear people around me express how disturbed they are about the state of things. That is not the energy a suffering world needs; it can deny your authentic self along with your spirit. You deserve to enjoy the life you have worked hard to create. It does not mean you don't care about the problems on earth. COVID was the most obvious example of this.

Some of the conversations between people went like this.

"This is so awful. I can't believe this is happening. Life sucks."

"Right, this is unbelievable. Tragic." The guilt was pervasive.

"Although. . . . I'm embarrassed to say it, and of course, I feel terrible for the people getting sick, but I haven't spent this much time at home in ages! Being rid of my busy schedule feels good."

"Right?! Phew, it's okay to be all right. I started baking up a storm. The kids LOVE my banana bread. I have even started painting again."

*Of course, no one was happy that people were sick and dying from COVID-19!* But did that mean they should be guilt-soaked? *Of course not.* Thank goodness they were okay and enjoying themselves, re-inventing themselves, and appreciating relationships they once took for granted!

Pain and joy can coexist. Black-and-white thinking is a thief of the precious, joyous moments life presents. We all have or will have unavoidable, heart-wrenching pain and loss in our lives. That is life. If we own everyone's pain all the time, life will be miserable. That's the difference between sympathy and empathy. We are not bad if we don't empathize with every person's plight or every crisis on the planet.

When we empathize, we are carrying the strife of our friend inside of ourselves. Our bodies dump cortisol and adrenaline into our systems. These cause nausea, sleeplessness, racing thoughts, and increased heart rates. This kind of behavior feeds and nurtures our anxiety and depression. The production of positive endorphins and neurotransmitters like serotonin and dopamine slow their production.

When we sympathize, for example, by giving someone a hug, we release oxytocin. It is known as the "cuddle hormone" which helps us to feel good and extends positive energy to the person you care for. By doing this you remain whole and healthy, becoming a good support system for your friend. You become a healer rather than a fellow sufferer.

Perhaps you know the kind of person who suffers so much for the pain of others that it causes people to refrain from sharing their difficulties with them because they are afraid of upsetting them. Or there are the types that will make the issue all about themselves. When someone's sadness is louder than the person who is hurting it is the opposite of helpful for everyone involved. Suffering more than the person who is in pain can be an unintentionally selfish act, forcing the person who was originally in pain to now soothe their caring friend.

When someone is hurting, they need the people around them to buoy their spirits, not jump in and drown with them. The way to be there emotionally for our friends, and the world around us, is to take care of ourselves, suck up every ounce of joy life presents, and be very exacting with the pain we choose to ingest. You must do this, or you can sicken yourself with anxiety over the tragedies up close and worldwide. You may instead opt to experience the beauty all around you as well. It is vital to you, your family, your friends, and the universe that you remain a helpful person who can add to the solutions, rather than become enveloped by the problems.

When you find yourself carrying the problems of others, take a moment to pause. Then you must make a conscious decision to release yourself from the pain. I find that when I hold the image of myself as a little girl, and I acknowledge all that little girl has been through in the past fifty-six years, it's easier for me to encourage her to go and enjoy her day. My Capable Adult Self wants me to experience every drop of pleasure that is available to me in life, and when I can imagine holding that little girl by the shoulders and telling her to go play, it assists me in freeing myself of worry. Then, just like in chapter 17, I pick an activity to focus on in the present moment. I use my surroundings and my five senses to redirect my thoughts and have a good day.

## Build Your Toolkit

Get your user manual.

1. In chapter 7, I asked you to find a picture of yourself as a young child, keep it next to your bed, and promise that child that you would love and protect it. Get that same picture now and put it in front of you.
2. Close your eyes.
3. Search your heart and your body for the pains you are carrying for others.
4. Each time one pops into your awareness, write it down.
5. Do this until the concerns in your life on are the page rather than in your body.
6. Now go back to the list.
7. How many degrees of separation exist between you and the pain you are holding for others?
8. Make a decision to give that little person in the photograph in the photo in front of you as much joy as you can. Choose to let go of all worries that have more than one degree of separation. You can still support the people who are suffering by listening and being there when it's appropriate, but you don't need to carry these anxieties and pains while you are not in the presence of these people.
9. Now revisit the list that has the people with one degree of separation. Is owning their pain helpful? If the answer is no, give yourself permission to be free of that too.
10. Now put that photograph back, right next to your bed. Every morning when you wake up promise your young self that you will not carry the problems of others and are going to help her/him/them the best day possible, no matter what.
11. Do that every morning until the thoughts to take care of yourself are hard-wired in your brain and become a regular part of your being.

CHAPTER TWENTY-ONE

~

# Embrace Plan B

"I'm sure it's no surprise to you. . . ." The ringing in my ears prevented me from hearing the rest of the sentence. *Is she really giving me the "you're fired" speech? The speech she taught me to use on the people she made ME fire?* I looked at Jennifer. Her mouth was moving, and her cropped, gelled hair was motionless. The deep red on the walls reflected my insides. *I thought we were building this treatment center together.*

In the past two years, I have gone from intern to Executive Clinical Director. Last week, on a trip to the spa, we spoke about opening a detox center together. *Today she was firing me?! It wasn't personal. This was Jennifer.*

"So, I'm the last one in the hot seat?" I said, needing to make this as quick as possible.

"I'm so sorry, Laura. Truly," she said.

I had ridden the financial roller coaster with her in the past. I was either paid a fortune or worked for free on more than one occasion. Working for free again was no longer an option. My neurofeedback practice was doing well, but it was only open two days a week, and there was no way we could live on that. My husband was working on a book, and it had been easy supporting us with income from both my jobs. *But what was I going to do now?*

"You know I wish you the very best of luck," is the next thing I heard her say.

"Of course." We hugged. The pleasantries were nauseating. Or was it the five thousand quarts of adrenaline spewing from my sympathetic nervous system?

I called my best friend. "Well, guess what just happened?"

"Uhhhh . . ." There was no point in letting her squirm; she would never guess.

"I just got fired," I said.

"WHAT? Are you serious?" I could feel the jolt of disbelief through the phone.

"Oh, quite," I said.

"Oh my God. I'm so sorry." She was.

"What are you doing right now?" I asked.

"Ummm, what do you want me to be doing?" A friend indeed.

"I don't know. Maybe just run away." There was a pause.

"Why don't we go have lunch in Ojai?" She knew me so well. Ojai was one of our sanctuaries and only an hour away. A town made up of hippies and wealthy seekers of peace. Its picturesque Topa Topa Mountains have been painted in their pink hue many times over by amateurs and famous artists compelled to capture Ojai's magic.

"I think that would be great. You're the best. What am I going to do?" My brain quantum leaped from the freedom of Ojai right back into doom.

"God's got your back. It's going to be okay. We've got this. Just come and pick me up." Grounding and calming words.

I called my sister to quiet the noise of my Wounded Child on the way to my friend's place.

"What's wrong?" She knew every tone of my emotions.

I spewed into her ear.

My sister interrupted, "Sisu, you always land on your feet. You have your master's degree now. Anyplace would be lucky to have you."

I grunted in feigned amusement. There was a long pause.

"You know . . ." I heard the lightbulb go on over her head.

"There are so many drug addiction places, but you are so good with anxiety. There aren't any anxiety places, are there? I bet you could start your own place and just focus on anxiety."

I was too numb to take her seriously. "I'm gonna take a drive to Ojai."

"Great idea. I love you so much. It's all going to be okay. Really." Her words were genuine.

My friend and I sipped our coffees as we waited for breakfast at good old Bonnie Lu's, a 1950s-style diner with red vinyl, comfy booths, and table caddies of ketchup, mustard, and maple syrup. The intoxicating smell of pancakes released serotonin into my nervous system and relaxed my gut.

"Want a refill, honey?" said the server, dressed in a worn-out pink uniform and nurse-like hat bobby-pinned to her head with a pen shoved behind her ear. Her tone was uplifting and sweet. She had been here as long as the booths.

"That'd be great," my friend answered.

She poured coffee and joy right into our cups.

"You are so happy," I said, almost surprised that someone could be happy right now.

She tipped her head back with a laugh, "May as well be!"

Words I needed to hear right then. *May as well be. Sage advice.*

My friend smiled at her and then at me, "Come on, let's think about a solution, not the problem. We're in Ojai; let's feel that energy."

"You know," I told her, "my sister had an idea that wasn't so bad. She pointed out that all of the treatment centers are drug rehabs, but there are no places that focus specifically on anxiety," I continued.

"Kay." She was with me so far.

My wheels started turning. "In my neurofeedback practice, I rent those two little offices out to other therapists, but what if I used one of the rooms for art therapy and another for movement, I'll bring in aromatherapy, and I'd love to offer massage. Head-to-toe anxiety treatment. I could do an Intensive Outpatient Program for anxiety."

She looked me in the eye, "Now we're talkin'."

My creation was forming bit by bit, "As a clinical director I learned how to bill insurance directly, and if patients are coming three days a week. I only need a fistful of patients to get me started. I'm pretty sure a couple of the patients would seek me out."

"See. This is the Laura I know!" Her head bobbed with excitement.

"This is crazy," My Wounded Child was worried, but my Capable Adult Self calmed her down, and my intuition was excited.

"Yes. And you're crazy. That's why I love you. You're the good kind of crazy." She laughed.

Now I was on a roll. "I already use the business name the Missing Peace for the neuro practice."

I tried to think of a name. Once I name it, it's real. After a few failed attempts, "How about the Missing Peace Center for Anxiety?" I could feel the excitement down to my toes.

She pointed her fork at me, "I love it."

That was on January 17, 2017. I opened a week later. By May the following year, the Missing Peace Center for Anxiety moved to a four-thousand-foot space, and my friend became my Director of Administration and Admissions. In May 2019, we expanded into the suite across the hall. Today, as I write this on June 18, 2022, the center is over ten thousand square feet of beautiful, healing, and much-needed anxiety treatment. No doom. No financial ruin. A dream come true.

## Anxiety User Manual: The Lesson, the Gift, and the Opportunity

One of the best things my mother taught me was that in every situation there is a lesson, a gift, and an opportunity. The curve balls life throws you are not meant to strike you out. They are meant to improve your game and make you a stronger member of the team. There is always something good that can be discovered through your pain. What's the best way to grow fruit? Manure. It's true that when you feel like you're buried in shit, start looking for the seeds that can be cultivated. You've heard the bumper stickers, "When one door closes, another one opens." "Rejection is Protection." "Look for the silver lining." "It's meant to be." There is a reason you've heard these sayings over and over. Because *they are true*. There is *always* a solution, and your Capable Adult Self knows that. Instead of going straight to doom it knows this so-called problem is about to create opportunity.

Every living entity is trying to grow and improve. That includes the universe. We can't always see the bigger picture. When the universe is pruning and designing itself, we are part of that grand design. We are meant to grow in new ways from our difficulties, not wither. Getting fired and being planted someplace else helped spread the availability of wellness. It's like the universe cut me from one healing tree and put me in new soil to grow roots and form another one.

A good way to build trust in your higher power is by following its lead, rather than shaking your fist in anger when you are dealt a card you do not want or were not expecting. Go with the flow and embrace plan B. It's nice to have a plan and watch it play out, but much-unneeded anxiety is born from a change of plans. When plans change, some people interpret that as a loss of control and panic at the idea of not knowing what's going to happen next. This concept presumes that we know it all, and we understand the bigger picture. We do not, and thank goodness there is something that does!

But it has taken me years to feel comfortable trusting the universe. When you first begin this practice, it is blind faith. Perhaps you are familiar with the phrase, "Leap and the net will appear." I disagree with that idea. When examined closely, it implies you will fall into the net! The saying should be, "Leap and you will fly." That is what real faith is about. The more you leap and fly, the more you will trust the journey.

If I had listened to my anxiety and focused on my fears instead of my intuition, my center would not have been created. It makes sense that losing my job would appear to my brain like "lion." But, instead of plummeting into despair, I paused, contacted the people that I trusted, and drove to an environment that would calm me down. It was only then that I could recognize that the "lion" was an amazing opportunity dressed in a lion costume. I found the lesson, the gift, and the opportunity. I embraced plan B, and it turned out that the universe had a bigger and better plan for me and the people I am now able to help.

## Build Your Toolkit

Get your user manual. Let's use my story as an example to identify the lesson, the gift, and the opportunity.

The Lesson: I could have recognized the ups and downs of Jennifer's business and not put so many of my eggs in her basket. I chose to ignore the instability.

The Gift: If it weren't for getting fired, I might never have opened the Missing Peace. It helped me find my true purpose, and it has become a gift to hundreds of people who have walked through its doors and found healing.

The Opportunity: I learned from the mistakes Jennifer encountered in growing her business, and I avoided those pitfalls in creating my center.

Think of a situation that you thought was going to become a disaster but ended up turning out for the best.

1. Make four columns: Plan A (the original plan that went wrong), Lessons, Gifts, and Opportunities.
2. Write the lesson in the corresponding column that came from a plan going wrong.
3. Write down the gift that came from plan B.
4. Write the opportunity that came from plan B.
5. Do this with three other events.
6. Now take a moment to acknowledge that the universe has a plan that works.
7. Consider going with the flow on the next plan B that arises for you, either big or small. It's a lot easier than kicking and screaming your way through it. You might miss the lesson, the gift, and the opportunity it has to offer.

# CHAPTER TWENTY-TWO

~

# Music Calms the Savage Beast

A woman in her forties sat across from me on my couch. Her shaking, nervous body cried into the cool, wet, lavender-soaked washcloth. As she wiped the tears from her eyes she looked up and met my gaze.

"Thank you. That made me feel a little better," she said with a quiet voice.

I replied in kind, "That's what I'm here for. I'm glad you came."

She settled into my sofa.

"How can I help?" I said. "What brought you to the Missing Peace?"

"I don't want to die, but I can't live like this anymore. My whole life is anxiety. I don't know who I am anymore. I'm driving my husband and my kids crazy. They don't know what to do for me. I've tried antidepressants, I've tried yoga, I feel like I've tried everything. My doctor said there is nothing wrong with me and told me I should get therapy, but I've tried that, and I'm sorry, I don't mean any disrespect, but therapy hasn't worked for me either. I mean, maybe a little, but. . . ." She covered her face with the washcloth again.

I chimed in, "I totally get it. Even though I think I'm a good therapist, I always tell my patients it takes more than flour to make cake. That's why I created the center. Would you like me to give you a little tour so I can better explain what I mean?"

She held up the washcloth, "Can I take this with me?" She followed with a nervous laugh.

"Absolutely! That's why I greeted you with it. Right away, I was able to engage two of your senses, smell and touch. The lavender scent is relaxing you, and the cool cloth is calming your nervous system as well."

I went on to explain further. "Listen, if your dog was really freaked out, you wouldn't say 'What triggered you, Fluffy?' You would try and soothe your pet. Even though we are all modern with our hoverboards and cellphones, we are still animals, right? Before we can think clearly about what's bothering us, we need to calm ourselves down. Your five senses are the best way to do that."

As she held the cloth to her nose, we started our walk through the facility. The halls were painted a buttery, creamy yellow. Fountains could be heard throughout the center, providing a sense of nature, and the typical office fluorescent lighting had been replaced with LED lights and gel covers designed to look as though you were staring up at trees, blue skies, and fluffy white clouds.

We stepped into a room decorated with a desk, two comfortable chairs, and a baker's rack full of aromatherapy. "The lavender you are smelling relaxes you, but lavender is only the tip of the iceberg. Most of us know it's supposed to help you to fall asleep, but sandalwood lets you *stay* asleep. Rosemary releases neurotransmitters in your brain that enable you to focus more clearly. Each essential oil triggers different neurotransmitters in your brain. The olfactory sense is the oldest and most developed sense in our bodies. Smells can change our brain chemistry and transport us instantly. Our specialist will create personalized scents for you to help you accomplish more relaxed states of being."

"That makes sense," she said, no pun intended.

Next, we stepped into a room dimly lit by twinkle lights with eight beds, various instruments, and a stage adorned with sound bowls.

Her eyes open wide. "This room is sooo cooool."

"Music calms the savage beast. We do music therapy here. It's not about playing an instrument; it is about releasing your anxiety and depression through sound. Sometimes we just beat drums or yell through a didgeridoo; even our bodies can make good percussion instruments. We also do sound baths to change the frequencies in your cells that are causing you tension and stress." I let her look around for a moment and then guided her gently across the hall.

"This is an art therapy studio. Don't worry, you don't need to be an artist, it's actually a little easier if you're not," I explained.

"Oh, thank God, because I'm a terrible artist!" She laughed.

I smiled at her. "Art creates avenues to express your trauma through a different part of your brain. The art therapist will guide you through therapeutic projects. We once had a woman who painted a birdhouse meant to represent who she was. It was all pink, but the roof was black. When she explained the color of the roof to the therapist she said, 'From now on, if anyone tries to look down on me, they will go into a void.'"

I went on, "She decided to set a boundary by creating a visual tool."

"I'm going to try and remember that," she said.

"Great! That's the idea." I led her into the next room.

"This is the horticulture therapy room." She stared at glass vases that aligned one of the walls, next to the flower and herb seeds.

I put my hand into the soil trough. "Soil releases serotonin, your feel-good neurotransmitter. Everyone gets to create a plant at the start of their treatment, they nurture it and watch it grow as they grow. Corny, I know, but people enjoy it."

She stared at me with a combination of awe and relief. "I can't believe you have all of these things here in one place. This is amazing."

"Thank you. Really. That's what I mean by it takes more than flour to make the cake. We want to work with your body, your mind, and your spirit to retrain your anxiety so that it works for you rather than against you."

"I know that's only four of your senses, but there is more to come." We continued the tour, which will continue in the following chapters.

## Anxiety User Manual: Come to Your Senses

I'm trying to reintroduce the phrase "come to your senses." In my day, it was Humphrey Bogart slapping some actress and saying, "Come to your senses, Doll," but the real trick to soothing your anxiety starts with your five senses. The four senses I addressed in the tour of the Missing Peace were smell, sight, sound, and touch.

I find it ironic that the key to escaping your anxiety is to "distract" yourself, when the truth of the matter is, *it is the anxiety that is the distraction*. When our anxiety is taking over, we become numb to our real senses, and the moment we are in. We are trapped in an imaginary doomsday scenario and are completely disconnected from our bodies. But, when three or more of your senses are engaged, you return to your body, and it becomes difficult for your brain to focus on your anxiety.

The specialist who does the aromatherapy at my center used to work at the St. John's Hospital cancer ward in Santa Monica. Her work focused on relieving nausea and creating calm for those undergoing chemotherapy treatments. She has taught me that essential oils are medicine. They change our brain chemistry in healthy and controllable ways.

I carry the scents she has designed for me with me at all times. Some relax me, some help me concentrate, but most of all, they keep me present and available for the task at hand. It is a simple way to assist my brain in keeping my Wounded Child calm and make room for my Capable Adult Self and intuition to experience the moment I am in, rather than get sucked down the rabbit hole.

Next up is sight. Based on a concept known as "biophila" my center is designed to look like you are in nature. Biophilia, suggests that connecting with nature brings positive feelings to human beings. When I ask my patients where they feel the most peace, nine times out of ten they speak of someplace in nature, such as the beach or the mountains. I've never understood why medical centers are so austere and cold. I get that they are supposed to look clean, but they are not all relaxing. The environment we encounter visually impacts how we feel. It sets the mood. If I'm going to see a doctor, I'd like to feel as relaxed as possible! I want my patients to feel comfort and connection.

We decorate our homes to help us feel a certain way and comfort ourselves with a unique taste and design that is personal to us. Colors evoke feelings. Red is often associated with danger. Green means nature. When people look upon a city, they experience different thoughts and feelings than when they look at a tropical island. Finding ways to visually relax yourself is an important part of coping with your anxiety.

Some people like to walk in the garden, some like to stare at a cozy fireplace, and even television is a way of using sight to steal yourself from an otherwise anxious mind.

When you are in a heightened state of anxiety, chances are you are not looking at what's in front of you. You are focused on imaginary worries in your mind's eye. You can use your eyes to concentrate on the objects surrounding you and bring yourself back to the present moment.

Now for some sound advice. Oh no I didn't. Okay, I did, but seriously, when your anxiety is screaming at you, seek sound to silence it. To get away from what's going on inside, you must connect with what's going on outside of your head. Kind of like fighting fire with fire. Sound is a great tool to combat the noise in your head and bring yourself back into the present moment.

There is something magical about music. It's like a time machine. Songs can transport you to a different time and place. They can change the way you feel. Why not use that to your advantage? Use music to change your mood, or at least get you to remember something positive, which will bring you closer to feeling better. If you're up for it, sing out loud and strong. Your very own voice, good or bad, will release anxious energy from your body and again help you focus on the voice that is in the moment, rather than the ones in your head. We do a lot of *singing out our frustrations* at the center.

Sound baths are a great method for distracting and soothing the anxious brain. Sound bowls when played emit sound waves that penetrate your cellular frequency and move you into a relaxed trance-like state, giving your brain the needed time off. They are best in person, but if none are available, listening to a sound bath should do the trick. There are so many apps that offer soothing sounds as well as calming voices that aid you in feeling better.

Calling a friend and hearing a comforting voice can be a good go-to when you're freaking out. Sometimes a voice at the other end of a hotline, a stranger who is waiting for your call and available twenty-four hours a day will be just the company you need to get you over an anxious hump. There is always *someone* who can talk to you, and quiet the worried voices in your head.

I personally love Audible. I have listened to over thirty books this year, sitting in traffic, trying to fall asleep, or just hanging in a hammock in my backyard. Podcasts, old-timey radio shows, apps, and music are some of the countless ways for your ears to pull you away from the noise of anxiety.

Last but not least, touch. One of the first things I teach my patients is that cool things will calm you down. Holding an icepack in your hand is a great tool for anxiety while you're sitting in a class, taking a test, or getting ready for some public speaking. No one can see it, it's easy to carry, and it soothes you right away.

If you're at home an icepack on your chest is an instant cool down, try a wet washcloth on your chest, or the back of your neck. As I mentioned in my story, every person who comes to the center is greeted with a cool lavender or eucalyptus cloth and it always brings them down a notch.

Walk your toes through the grass. Feel the energy of the earth through your feet. There is wonderful energy pouring through the earth's surface, that will soothe you and ground you. Most of our nerve endings are in our feet. They are a great place to put essential oils as well. Make sure that they are meant to go on the body and not the kind used to freshen a room.

Put your hands in some dirt! Or in the sand! Swim in a pool or the ocean. Get in touch with nature literally. I have a Zen Garden at the center that patients love to wander through.

Rosary beads and touchstones are ancient methods of touch known to aid in comfort and of course, one of the most soothing things in the world is human touch. A hug can go a long way, and that includes a hug you give to yourself.

You will find it very difficult to think about anything else when you have activated at *least three* of your senses. Our brains are not as good at multitasking as we think. Whatever you are thinking about right now, or worried about will become difficult to connect with if you try the exercise below.

## Build Your Toolkit

I want you to try an experiment using three of your senses.

1. Find a smell or taste you find soothing such as essential oil, perfume, a flower, suntan lotion, chocolate-chip cookie, a mint, or coffee.
2. Now find something you like to listen to such as music, guided meditation, or an audiobook.
3. Lastly, find something visually pleasing such as a fireplace, a tall tree, a piece of art, a picture of something that makes you happy, or even a pretty screensaver of a place you'd like to be.
4. Once you have those items, focus on all three things at the same time. Stare at the beauty while you smell or taste your chosen delight, and tune in to the sound. You may need to keep a rotation going if it's hard to focus on more than two. You will see that your other thoughts will be held at bay as long as you keep at least three senses engaged.
5. Now pick different choices and do the whole exercise a second time.

# CHAPTER TWENTY-THREE

~

# The Body Electric

As we continued the tour, I showed the patient the brain and body area of the Missing Peace and invited her to sit in one of the large leather, neurofeedback recliners that faced a large television monitor.

Holding her now warm washcloth out to me, she said, "I think I'm done with this now."

"Good." I took it from her and put it in a nearby towel bin.

I continued, "The tools of the senses are to help you in the moment. The brain and body center are about long-term changes. Neurofeedback is going to make changes to your limbic system. Right now, it is overwhelmed and hypervigilant, but neuro will slowly remove all the proverbial straws from the amygdala's back so that everything stops seeming like a 'lion' and you no longer become hijacked by your emotions. I will go into detail about how it works when you start your treatment."

She looked up at me. "I'm not sure I understand completely, but if you can stop my emotions from hijacking me, I don't even need to understand it. I'll just be glad to feel normal again."

I nodded. "I know it's a lot to take in all at once, but I promise you will understand everything that's happening here once you get going."

"Super," she said, as we went into the next room.

"This is the Pulse Electronic Magnetic Field therapy room. If you can say that backward you are instantly cured."

We both laughed a little.

I went on, "Humor, good and bad, is also part of the treatment here. If you're not laughing and only crying, we are doing something wrong."

"That would be great, I miss laughing," she said.

"Oh god, I so remember that feeling." My heart went out to her. "You will laugh again, I promise."

I pointed back to the machine in the room. "We call this the PEMF room for short. When we have inflammation or scar tissue in our bodies, the frequencies in our cells are not connecting and communicating which causes energy blockage and interrupts flow inside of our bodies. With PEMF you can just sit back in that comfy recliner and watch something soothing on the monitor. The gold plates are placed on blocked areas and held there gently with Velcro. They will adjust your cellular frequency and reinvigorate flow. Again, I'll explain more about it when you start."

"Wow, I've never even heard of this stuff," she said.

"Yeah, big pharma wants you on pills; the good stuff is kept on the down low," I answered.

I showed her into a room that mimicked the feeling of nighttime. The panels on the ceiling were painted like the night sky and glistened with lights that did a good job of imitating stars. Planet murals covered the walls. I pointed to the massage table in the center of the room. "This is the massage/alpha-stim room."

"Yes, please," she said.

"Right?" I continued. "You will get a massage every week and while you are getting your massage, you will be hooked up to an alpha-stim, which looks like a small MP3 player with two clip-ons for your ears. It will help your brain waves switch from an active beta state to a more mellow alpha state. This way your brain and your body become relaxed in synchrony."

"Sounds good to me," she said.

"Me too." I chuckled. "The whole staff tries to get time in here! We have to practice what we preach."

At this point we stepped into a large movement room with yoga mats and foam rollers. "Now as much as we want to be relaxed, we also want to move that anxious energy around and get it out of your body.

In this room we do gentle yoga moves, nothing strenuous. We also do breathwork."

"That's so weird you said that because I catch myself *not* breathing all the time," she said as we passed through to the next room.

I responded, "I used to catch myself holding my breath too." We continued down the hallway.

"Next stop is the nutrition kitchen." I swept my arm in front of me like Vanna White on a game show.

"Our health coach will teach you about primary food and secondary food. Primary food is not the food you put on your plate. It is the emotional energy that is feeding you. Whatever you're taking in spiritually determines what you put on your plate to eat. That is the secondary food. Does that make sense for now?"

"I think so." She looked at all the kitchen equipment. "My appetite is all over the place. I'm either overeating or I can't eat at all."

"Our stomachs are one of the first things to go off kilter with anxiety. The other big one is sleep," I said.

"Yes! I have so much trouble sleeping," she said exasperated.

I reassured her. "Don't worry, all this, and especially the neuro, is going to help with your sleep."

"That I'll believe when I see it. I've always had trouble sleeping. My doctor gave me Ativan, but it only works sometimes," she explained.

I empathized, "Ugh. I had sleep problems my whole life, but not anymore. Your body knows how to sleep when it's settled and functioning properly."

"If I do fall asleep," she continued, "it's early in the morning and then I wake up in panic with the worst feeling of dread."

"That's the perfect segue into the next area of the center." I guided her across the hall.

## Anxiety User Manual: More Ways That Your Body Can Quiet Your Anxiety

*Neurofeedback*

My whole company started with neurofeedback. So, let's start with that. It is a game changer, and it's a little hard to explain, even though it's the easiest therapy you can do. If patients can only do one modality because of cost or insurance, I always recommend neurofeedback.

Here's how neurofeedback works. Your brain is amazing. If you have a cut on your leg right now, your brain is repairing it. You are not even aware that is happening, but it is. The brain fixes everything in the body and the way it does that is through your nerve endings. Everything in your body is connected to nerve endings and they send signals through your spinal cord and up to your brain. Your brain gets the message and sends a signal back down about how to handle it and what to do next.

The irony is the brain itself does not have nerve endings. When surgeons do brain surgery, quite often the patient is awake and communicating with the doctor. Of course, the patient is sedated, but the doctor can map brain function to know what important areas to avoid removing. So here is this master organ that can fix everything but itself!

About ninety years ago, some neuroscientists thought, what if the brain could see and hear itself? Would it self-repair? The answer turned out to be yes, and neurofeedback was born. Five electrodes are placed on the surface of the scalp. This is called an electroencephalogram (EEG). You are probably familiar with an electrocardiogram (EKG). Maybe you've seen it on medical shows. The patient has stickers on their chest that are each connected to a wire, and you can see a pen moving up and down on a chart that shows the electrical activity of the heart. These electrodes *do not* send electric currents to the heart. It is the opposite. They are reading the electrical activity of the heart and sending it to the moving chart.

This is what's being done with the EEG. For our purposes, we are reading the electrical activity of the limbic system, the emotion center. That information then goes into our computer and gets projected onto the television monitor in front of the patient, while they sit comfortably in the recliner chair.

When I first started administering neuro, my patients would watch fractal images of their brains on the monitor. The patient watched flashing imagery resembling bad Pink Floyd meets Spirograph. This is what the patient's "mind" sees. Meanwhile, the brain interprets this information differently. For the brain, it's like looking in a mirror. The brain can read the movement and perceive its own behavior through the moving imagery. The brain then fixes the dysfunction it sees.

When we look in the mirror, we naturally fix whatever we see that is out of place. We are not the only animals that do this. There is something called "The Rouge Test" in which rouge is put on the subject's face—that is, human, rat, bird, or ape—and the subject is put in front of a mirror. The subject instinctively wipes the rouge off of its face.

The brain functions the same way. It can see that the limbic system is overwhelmed, and it starts to repair itself. It systematically goes through its own trauma file cabinet and starts to put things in a safe place. This is not a quick fix. It can take twenty to eighty sessions, but it is a long-term change. Your brain does not revert to its previous state unless you are subjected to a lot more trauma. Many patients come in for a tune-up once a year or so. Some say they don't need it.

Since I have started treating people with neurofeedback, the technology has been updated, and instead of looking at fractal images directly, those images get encoded into whatever movie is chosen by the patient. They can pick from any selection from Netflix and away they go. Easiest therapy ever. Sit back, watch a movie, and let your brain fix itself.

There are those in the medical field who dismiss neurofeedback, which is a shame. Not only have I seen it change hundreds of people's lives, including my own, but it is used by NASA to help their astronauts stay focused and be calm in space. Sports teams use it because if you are overthinking, you're most likely to miss your shot, and most importantly, the American Pediatric Association considers neurofeedback the *most effective and recommended* treatment for ADD and ADHD. It has also offered ground-breaking healing for the autistic community.

### Pulse-Electronic Magnetic Field Therapy

PEMF is another modality that has brought me tears of joy. I had a patient who could not walk due to severe pain from an ectopic pregnancy, and within ten sessions she reported dancing in the shower. It works by sending magnetic waves of energy that encourage your own magnetic energy to realign in a healthy flow. It is very effective for chronic pain and also for depression. It increases the healthy charges in your ions and boosts your electrolytes. Therefore, dysfunctional electric currents within the body are converted into normal states of flow and being. PEMF helps the body to recover, and it gives you more energy. Again, sit back and relax while your body heals.

### Massage

Who doesn't love a good massage? The obvious benefit of massage is relaxation, but it does so much more. Whether it is a small amount of stress or a serious event traumatic energy gets trapped in our muscles. Our body's health benefits greatly from a good massage. Just like PEMF, massage releases blocked energy trapped in your muscles, helps your heart rate, calms you down, improves circulation, and reduces cortisol levels known as the stress hormone. It also boosts your immune system.

Massage is an important modality for the treatment of depression and anxiety because it increases the flow of blood to your brain and releases dopamine and serotonin, the feel-good neurotransmitters.

### Movement

I may be stating the obvious, but, of course, movement is an accessible elixir in aiding anxiety and depression. It doesn't have to be anything strenuous. A simple, ten-minute walk can do a lot for our brain health.

Aside from the benefit of movement itself, we do light yoga at the center because it engages more than one of your senses. It takes some concentration to find the position and hold it, which brings you into the moment! It quiets the great distraction we call, yes, anxiety. There is music playing and the practitioner's voice gently guides the patients as they focus on body positions and the feel of the mat. Movement is used to teach patients another method of connecting to the present and quieting their anxiety.

### Nutrition

Comfort food has been a go-to for me ever since I can remember. When my husband and I first got married, if one of us came home and said, "We are ordering pizza," the other knew *someone had a hard day*. We both seemed to crave pizza when we were stressed. For me, boredom can lead to unhealthy eating. But is it comfort food? In some ways, yes. Most comfort foods have carbohydrates. Carbs are loaded with serotonin. Our brain doesn't care how we get this feel-good neurotransmitter, it just wants to feel good, even if the body doesn't afterward. Therefore, it follows that what we are feeling spiritually is going to impact what we put in our bodies.

The four basic categories our nutrition expert focuses on are self-care, relationships, career, and health. When one or more of those are out of balance, or dysfunctional, it will likely impact what we choose to eat.

In the next chapter we will look at the spiritual modalities used at the Missing Peace. In the meantime, let me suggest some ways you can find some of the aforementioned therapies near you.

## Build Your Toolkit

Finding a neurofeedback provider near you is easy. I use a technology called Cygnet. Different practitioners may use different equipment. If you are not noticing any difference, even slight ones, in the first five sessions, perhaps try someone else.

1. Go to eeginfo.com; select "find a provider" and then enter your zip code.
2. I recommend checking reviews and feeling comfortable with the practitioner. Don't be shy about meeting some first until you find someone you trust.

For PEMF providers I have given you a WebMD link to assist you in finding one in your area: https://doctor.webmd.com/providers/procedure/pulsed-electromagnetic-field-pemf.

Massage near you is available. Again, don't be afraid to try different therapists until you find one you like. Some will even come to you! While massage can be pricey, I have found several foot massage places that will do a whole-body massage for thirty dollars. You will be fully clothed and in a room with others, but I have gotten many a good massage at these types of venues. The foam rollers we use in the movement room can be found for ten bucks on Amazon and you can use them to massage yourself.

The type of movement you select is personal. Different approaches work for different people. Just get your body moving and make sure you are engaging two more of your senses. I know how hard it is to do these things with depression. Small steps will do just fine, but twenty anxiety-fueled jumping jacks, push-ups, or sit-ups really helps! Here are some other ideas.

1. The easiest one is going for a walk. You can listen to something or focus on the sounds around you while you visually take in your environment.
2. If you're on a treadmill, watch TV or listen to music while you're doing it.
3. Zumba or dancercise is a good one and it's a fun way to be in the moment. Or just turn on some music and dance your heart out for ten minutes.
4. I like this link for a small morning stretch, but there are many short or long workouts and stretches available on youtube.com: https://www.youtube.com/watch?v=ihba9Lw0tv4
5. Hit a bucket of golf balls.
6. Shoot some hoops. Don't stop until you make ten baskets.

Get your user manual. Create a section for spirituality and nutrition.

1. Write down the last meal you ate.
2. How did you feel before you ate it?
3. Did your mood make your food choice for you?
4. Plan your next meal thoughtfully.
5. Do a gratitude prayer for well-being before you choose the food.
6. Create time for it without rushing.
7. Think of a pleasant space in which to have it like an outside table on your patio, in front of the fireplace, or if you are making yourself a meal, set the table for yourself, maybe even a candle.
8. Do a gratitude prayer before you eat it.
9. When you're finished, write about the experience in your user manual.

# CHAPTER TWENTY-FOUR

~

# Energy Matters

"This is where east meets west." Our tour continued. "No matter how many times I see the amazing results these modalities produce, there is still a skeptical voice inside of me. But this is all science. Energy is science and so is energy work."

She interjects, "Oh, no, I love this stuff. My sister is not into it, but I am."

I shared a story with her. "We once had a guy in here who owned a plumbing company. He was a skeptic, to say the least. As he left this room after his first session, his hair was tousled, and his eyes had a dreamy, far-off look."

He said, "I don't know what the hell just happened in there, but whatever it is, I like it and I want more."

She clapped her hands together with excited anticipation.

"Our Reiki specialist is magical. After she works on you, you'll feel like a different person. She is the same woman who does the aromatherapy. You will work with her quite a bit. She'll help you set intentions for yourself, and she also does HeartMath. She will explain it to you in detail during your session."

"Sounds cool," she said.

I led her into an office adorned with crystals, Buddha tapestries, and salt lamps. "The practitioner who does the sound baths, movement, and breathwork also does individual sessions with people. She uses guided meditation and hypnotherapy to facilitate patients in changing their 'story.' We often go through the same difficulties over and over again, because it has been our experience and therefore, we expect it to be like that always. But we can rewrite the scripts of our lives by letting go of old, dysfunctional stories and changing our energy."

"I'm all for that," she said.

I next invited her to take off her shoes and walk with me through the Himalayan salt and sand garden. It glimmered pink and beige, as we sat in the Adirondack chairs and ran our toes through the sand.

"How do you feel about meditation?" I asked.

She let out a heavy sigh. "I know it's supposed to be good for you, but it's so hard for me to do. I've tried it a few times, but I just can't seem to get into it."

I smiled. "I completely identify with that. I actually used to hate it. It was so frustrating. But it is a practice, not a perfect. There is no wrong way to do it and you have probably done it without even realizing it."

Her brow furrowed.

I continued, "Meditation by definition is simply a focus on something to understand it more deeply. For instance, surfing can be a meditation, gardening can be a meditation, even crossword puzzles can be a form of meditation."

"I didn't know that. I wish I knew that years ago," she replied.

"It's true. When you think of someone sitting cross-legged and chanting it too is meditation, but it is only one kind. A lot of people think it's about banishing all of your thoughts and thinking nothing, which is great if you are a yogi on a mountain top, but for me, meditation is about making friends with your brain and your thoughts."

She asked, "How do you mean?"

"Anxiety and depression speak loudly through our thoughts, and they have nothing uplifting to say. It's like having a terrible travel agent inside of your head."

"Oh my gosh, yes!" she squealed.

"Every practitioner here teaches a different type of meditation. They teach you how to make your brain a friendly place. Guided meditation is a great way to start meditation practice. The act of listening to someone and embarking on an imaginary journey, teaching you how to go anywhere you want, anytime, all by yourself."

She chimed in, "Those I've done. They're nice."

"They are the beginnings of having access to changing your thoughts and quieting your anxiety."

She buried her face in her hands and started crying again.

I held a quiet space for her to let out her sadness. Then I reached out and touched her shoulder. "It's going to be okay. I'm glad you're here."

She nodded as she continued to hold her face in her hands.

Once she was more relaxed, I said, "Let's go and talk for a bit."

She got up and followed me back to my private office.

## Anxiety User Manual: Changing Your Energy and Making Friends with Your Brain

*Reiki*

I discussed in the spiritual awakening chapter the importance of changing your energy. Sometimes it's nice to have help. For those of you unfamiliar with Reiki, let me shed some light on it. Reiki found its origins in Esoteric Buddhism. It means "universal life force." While acupuncture moves your energy with needles, Reiki moves energy with energy. Imagine that a professional energy worker is standing above you while you lay on a massage table. Instead of massaging your physical body, they are massaging your energy body. They are raising your frequencies. You have a physical body, *and* you have an energy body. There are many words for the energy body. Some call spirit, prana, soul, source, Qi (pronounced chee). There are numerous names for it, but they all refer to the energy body. Reiki workers clear blockages in your energy field by the magnetic force of their own healing hands. They work with all of your chakras and the magnetic fields in your energy body, cleansing, clearing, and lifting them.

*Intention Setting*

Because the woman who works with my patients is a master with energy, she is also skilled in directing and changing the path you are on. She helps you to set intention; to design your life with purpose.

When you listen to that little voice inside, your direction becomes illuminated, and setting your mind to achieve those goals requires focus.

Intention setting can be taken day by day, hour by hour, or minute by minute. It means to alert you to live the moments of your life to the fullest and aim at achieving your highest good. It helps you to course correct. Even a rocket that goes into space has a built-in system for course correction. It is natural to move off course. Intention setting keeps you on point with your goals.

## HeartMath

HeartMath is a technology used to provide insight into how much your thoughts impact your body. This kind of direct connection encourages patients to change their thought processes. Sure, I can tell you that when you imagine the worst-case scenario it affects your body, but when you can actually watch your heart rate change as your thoughts change, it has a much stronger impact.

Clip-ons attach to your ears while the practitioner guides you through different aspects of your life, and you can see on the computer screen how your pulse changes when your thoughts change. It strengthens the holistic concept of our body, mind, and spirit. Everything is connected. Everything is one. Seeing it makes it more tangible.

## Hypnotherapy

Whether you think so or not *you have been hypnotized*. Don't believe me? Have you ever watched TV? Television moves your brain into an alpha state, making you "suggestible." We will discuss alpha states in the chapter about sleep, but for now, take my word for it, TV leaves you open to suggestions. Therefore, when a commercial comes on showing a nice cool beer being consumed by a smiling person on a tropical beach—suddenly, a beer sounds pretty good. That is because when your brain is in an alpha state you are much more open to changing your behavior. Years ago, movie theaters used to cut quick clips of popcorn and soda into the film being watched, that were undetectable to the conscious mind, but very connected to the subconscious mind. It was called subliminal advertising and is now illegal, but it made people get up during the movie and buy the concessions. The next time you are at the grocery store, look up toward the higher part of the walls. They are adorned with tantalizing pictures of fresh produce, baked goods, and other trappings offered at your local market. They are targeting your subconscious mind and it works.

Believe it or not, guided meditation and hypnosis are not that far apart. You should understand that all hypnosis is self-hypnosis. The therapist, the commercial, or the market are merely facilitating suggestions while your brain is open to them. If you hate beer, the commercial is not going to make you want beer. If you want to quit smoking, hypnotherapy can work. If you don't, it most likely won't.

A hypnotherapist, through guided meditation, will put you into a relaxed state so you will be open to changing behavior that does not serve you. You are awake. Just very calm. The critical voice will be judging away in the background, but a good therapist helps that voice to become impotent and can connect with your subconscious if you are willing and open to the change being suggested.

### Meditation

Last, but not least, meditation. The conduit into your higher self and your connection to the universe. It is all one thing. We are in everything and everything is in us. Eastern philosophy and physics understand this idea. The difference is Eastern philosophy "senses" it and physics writes it out with mathematical symbols. To put it simply, Eastern thinking believes everything is one. Scientists seek to understand the connections of very tiny things as individual entities, which sometimes fails to see the bigger picture. Newtonian Law is applicable only until we get down to atomic size, then the rules no longer apply. To science the bigger picture must be understood before it can be believed.

Let's start with guided meditation. To the naked eye, it looks like you're lying on a couch or a bed, listening to some voice. But the visualization you have in your mind has nothing to do with your physical surroundings. The same thing occurs with anxiety. To the naked eye, you are on your couch or your bed, but the mental story you are experiencing has you someplace else. Somewhere scary and unmanageable, right? Meditation teaches to you take that magical transportive power and use it for happiness and connection rather than doom. Your mind is the best travel agent you can have.

Meditation means many different things. Just like you have been hypnotized, and didn't know, you have also meditated. As I mentioned in the story, playing golf can be a kind of meditation. The same is true of surfing, skiing, scrapbooking, crossword puzzles, gardening, and cooking. When you are immersed in an activity, your senses are engaged, and it's like nothing else is around you. These kinds of active meditations are wonderful avenues away from anxiety and depression.

Most people associate meditation with sitting cross-legged in a yoga position. Guess what? You don't even have to sit that way! Get comfortable! Lying down also works for meditation. The purpose of inward meditation is not to cut off from thought. It is to become one with everything and merge with the sound around you, the cushions below you, and the universe you are a part of!

If it's this kind of meditation you want to try, you've probably heard focusing on your breathing helps. It does. Another way to intensify the focus on your meditation is by staring at your third eye point. When your eyes are closed, focus on the point between your two eyebrows. That is your third eye point. This will help your thoughts from wandering. Give yourself some time. You can start slowly doing five to ten minutes at first and working your way up comfortably.

Morning meditation is the one I recommend the most. Do you ever notice that you wake up anxious? Even if you have nothing stressful in the day ahead, anxiety is happy to greet you before you can open your eyes. Thanks, anxiety. Not. The last two hours of our sleep cycle is the time our subconscious processes our stressors. This is why we often wake up anxious. Your brain doesn't know the difference between reality and virtual reality, so your nervous system is raring to go before your eyes have even opened. Many Yoga practices involve waking up early before that cycle takes place.

I believe it's important to let your brain process what it needs to process. Nothing against those practices, maybe I just like my sleep. But that's why morning meditation is so revered. It is a chance to quiet the anxiety and bring your brain back to harmony after processing stressors in your sleep. It's also easier to achieve trance states since you've just left a deep sleep state of being during sleep. It's a wonderful way to connect with answers that just seem to pop into your intuitive mind.

## Build Your Toolkit

Get your user manual.

1. Write down the intention you are hoping to achieve by reading this book.
2. Every morning when you wake up, get your manual, and write down your intention for the day ahead. Write what you'd like to achieve and how you want to feel while accomplishing your goals.

   Examples:

   Relax, spend time lying in the backyard, and feel peaceful.

   Or meditate, get to the market, write my paper, return some calls, and feel stress-free while I'm doing it.
3. Create a space in your house for meditation. It can be a whole room, a place outside, or even a small corner. Place some things there that you associate with spirituality. You can be as elaborate or minimalistic as you'd like. The goal is to make the space yours and to make it inviting.
4. Decide to start meditation practice. Pick any kind you like! Give yourself at least five minutes a day to sit and connect with your higher power and your intuition.
5. Here are some meditations to try:

   Vacation Meditation: In your mind's eye (your imagination) go to your favorite place to take a trip, or even pick a place you want to go but have never been to. Imagine what you would be wearing from head to toe. Imagine what you'd see 360 degrees around you, imagine what you'd smell, what you'd hear, feel the air temperature on your skin, imagine tasting something. Immerse yourself in the chosen vacation spot. If your mind wanders, go back to dressing yourself from the feet up and start again.

   Rainbow Meditation: Imagine you are walking through a rainbow. See the colors change around you and attach a positive feeling to each color you walk through. Take your time and let the sensations reach every cell in your body.

Beach Your Problems Meditation: Imagine you are standing on a beach, feel the sand and sun, and hear the surf and the seagulls. As the water laps gently over your toes, think of your problems one at a time. Imagine each one turns into a grain of sand and drops out of your head onto the beach. Let the water wash every problem away. Then find a sand cave and carve your blessing into the wall of the cave. Leave room for the blessings that are to come.

Third Eye Point Exercise: If you have trouble getting started, just sit and close your eyes. Don't do anything but close your eyes and become aware of how your mind jumps all over the place, and then notice that your eyes dart all around as well. After a minute or two, focus on your third eye point and notice that your mind will be quieter when your eyes are still.

These are the meditations I've created, and you can listen to them on the link I have included: https://www.amazon.com/Missing-Peace -Guided-Relaxation-Meditations-Rhodes/dp/B003YI1QR6

There are so many meditations available out there. Keep looking until you find one that works for you. You may find your taste changing and your skills revolving over time.

1. HeartMath is awesome! If you want to check it out, go to https:// www.heartmath.com/
   You can do it on your own with the HeartMath app and by the purchase of the sensors.
2. If Reiki or hypnotherapy interests you then let your fingers do the walking and google some therapists. As usual, do your homework, meet with different people, and make sure you feel comfortable with whom you opt to work with.

# CHAPTER TWENTY-FIVE

~

# I'd Rather Not Do Groups

We sat back down in my office. She snuggled into the couch and wrapped the blanket around herself.

"Have you got any questions for me?" I asked.

"What about actual talk therapy?" she queried.

"Of course, we do that, too. Most of the center is about developing self-soothing tools so that you are free to talk about your issues and are relaxed and trusting enough to approach your problems free of emotional hijacking. Talk therapy is important as well."

She nodded.

"I am lucky to have every therapist that works here. They are all different, and we will assign you one that we think is going to be best suited for your issues and your personality. They all specialize in different schools of thought like EMDR, brainspotting, CBT, DBT, and psychotherapy, but each uses a combination of different techniques, trusting their gut to read what you need at any given moment during the session."

"I'd like to try different kinds. I haven't even heard of some of those," she said.

"Your therapist will guide you to the ones that will work for you, based on the issues you are facing. You will also participate in several group sessions during your nine hours a week."

She shook her head. "I don't like groups."

I grinned. "Go over to my desk and open the white envelope sitting on top of it."

She walked over and picked up an envelope that looked less than brand new.

"This one?" she said holding up the envelope.

"That's the one. What does it say on the outside?" I asked.

She read aloud, "The one thing is . . ."

She looked up. "That's all it says."

"Now open it and read what's written on the paper inside."

She complied. "I'd rather not do groups."

I smiled at her. "You're not the only one who feels that. I keep that envelope on my desk every time I do a tour. About 85 percent of the time, it gets opened."

"Oh my gosh." She blushed.

"Most people want nothing to do with group therapy, but with some time you will see the benefits and may find yourself making friends with the other people in your group. It ends up being comforting to know you're not the only one who struggles and hurts in the same way you do."

She walked back to the couch and sat down.

"Everything here is put together with purpose and thought. Most people don't want to leave even after insurance stops paying for it."

"I'll probably be one of those people. I really hope this works." She looked me in the eye.

"I can't make you any promises, but in my experience, it works very well." I smiled.

## Anxiety User Manual: Talk Therapy at My Center

I'll take this opportunity to give you a brief description of some of the therapies I mentioned during the tour part of the chapter.

*Eye Movement Desensitization and Reprocessing*

Eye movement desensitization and reprocessing (EMDR) is a treatment designed to help patients with PTSD. Painful memories are recalled aloud as the therapist guides the patient to engage in an external activity that causes the brain to jump back and forth between the left and right hemispheres during the recall. For example, as the patient recites the trauma, they follow the therapist's finger moving left to right in their field of vision. Some therapists use vibrating handheld devices or do hand tapping instead. The layman's idea behind it is that when we experience trauma it does not get a chance to get stored properly in our brains, so it floats around and can get triggered at any point in time that reminds the person of the trauma. With the aid of EMDR the experience gets filed away to a safe place and trauma symptoms and stress no longer get activated.

### Brainspotting

Brainspotting was created by David Brand and is a popular new therapy on the trauma scene. We have found it to be very effective at the Missing Peace. Similar to EMDR, it involves recounting your trauma. But instead of the therapist directing your eye movement, they will notice where your eyes go when you experience heightened emotion in the retelling of your story. When you focus on that spot, it releases the emotional trauma associated with the story you are remembering.

### Cognitive Behavorial Therapy

Cognitive behavioral therapy (CBT) is just like it sounds. Your cognitions, or thoughts, will create your behavior. If you think a lion is chasing you, you run. Since many of our anxious and depressed thoughts are creations of neuroses or Wounded Child, CBT will help you look at your problems through the eyes of Capable Adult Self. It helps you see that it is a person in a lion outfit or not a real lion of any sort. As your thoughts change, your behavior follows. When you no longer fear an object your actions toward it become healthy, productive, and functional.

### Dialectical Behavioral Therapy

Dialectical behavioral therapy (DBT) is often used with bipolar patients and Borderline Personality Disorders, but I find it to be helpful for patients with extreme anxiety. It addresses black-and-white thinking. I wish gray was associated with a more uplifting feeling because most of life happens in the gray. Anxiety makes people think in extremes. Reprogramming thought distortions such as all-or-nothing thinking, overgeneralization, catastrophizing, or labeling are addressed with the help of the four elements of DBT, which are mindfulness, emotion regulation, interpersonal effectiveness, and distress tolerance.

## Psychotherapy

Mothers got star billing in the work of Sigmund Freud. Our primary caregivers play a large role in who become. We are products of our parents' teachings. Revisiting our childhood experiences, even if we think they are perfect, often explains a lot of our dysfunctional behavior and unhealthy life patterns. Connecting the dots to our seeds and roots does a lot to explain the kind of flower we have become. This is not an attempt to malign the people who raised you, as I demonstrated in chapters 1, 2, and 3, and most people are doing their best with the messed-up methods in which they were raised. The hope is that therapy addresses the dysfunction so it stops getting passed down, and the parts of your upbringing that no longer serve you can be removed from your thoughts and behaviors.

## Group

One of the reasons that twelve-step programs are so successful is that at their core, they are a support group. No one can understand you as well as someone who has had the same or similar experiences as you have had. When you have experienced a death in the family, a grief group is an excellent way to process the pain of losing a loved one.

As a therapist, I can sympathize with my patients. But if that patient is struggling with her cancer treatment, a support group filled with people who are navigating the same trials and tribulations either now or in the past is what I will recommend to her. No one wants to feel like they are alone and that nobody can understand what they are going through. Support groups connect you to fellow travelers who are empathetic with the painful journey you are on.

I provide the opportunity for the patients at my center to connect and relate to each other through group therapy. Group therapy saves individuals from having to reinvent the wheel that delivers them to happy and healthy healing. The others in the group convey the message, "We can help you with anxiety because we too suffer from it and understand your pain. We want to give you the tools that worked for us because they can help you too."

## Combining All of the Modalities

Getting back to the cake analogy, "it takes more than flour to make cake," the ingredients must be used together to work. If you put eggs in the oven, you don't get cake; same with the flour, sugar, milk, or even that one-eighth teaspoon of vanilla (God forbid you don't use the vanilla). You can't shove them in the oven separately and expect to make a cake. You need to use all the ingredients, with the right balance to get the desired result.

When you *combine* the aforementioned therapies from the last three chapters into one holistic approach, you get a wonderful recipe for balance and joy in body, mind, and spirit.

# Build Your Toolkit

### Finding Therapy

Here are some symptoms of trauma. If you find these apply to you, seek out trauma-specific therapy such as EMDR and brainspotting.

1. Flashbacks of a traumatic event cause you to experience intrusive thoughts that cannot be controlled.
2. The world no longer feels like a safe space.
3. Nightmares about the traumatic event.
4. Severe anxiety.

Enter your information on this link and you can find an EMDR therapist in your neighborhood: https://www.emdr.com/SEARCH/.

Here is the link to find a brainspotting therapist: https://brainspotting.com/directory/certified-bsp-therapists/.

If you are interested in finding a therapist for CBT, DBT, or psychotherapy, Psychology Today, www.psychologytoday.com, lists therapists in your area and you can indicate the type of therapy you are seeking.

Group therapy is more specific and specialized, but thanks to the internet you can find a support group that meets your needs. Here is a good link to get you started or help you learn about what group therapy can do for you on a more complex level: https://www.helpguide.org/articles/therapy-medication/support-groups.htm.

# CHAPTER TWENTY-SIX

~

# The Sleep Dilemma

"Earlier in the tour, you mentioned sleeping better." The patient continued, "You have no idea how hard it is for me to sleep. I am exhausted all the time, and no matter what I do, it doesn't help."

"Believe it or not, I understand it on a personal level. Let me share with you a bit of my battle with sleep. It has a good ending."

"Okay, that would be great," she said.

I shared, "I struggled with sleep my whole life. I was born with anxiety that kept me awake. I was so grateful in my thirties when they invented Ambien, but sometimes it worked and sometimes I would wake up to string cheese wrappers that I did not remember opening during the night."

She jumped in, "Oh my God, I can't believe you said that. Ambien made me do weird things too!"

"Right?" I acknowledged. "I became reliant on any pill that would help me sleep, but they never really worked completely, because my brain kept me awake and I would develop a tolerance."

She nodded in agreement.

I reassured her, "It's not that your body can't sleep, it's that your anxiety is producing the opposite effect. In the long run sleep meds suck for sleep, because they train your brain to believe that you can't sleep without them and your body becomes addicted to them."

"Believe me, I know," she said.

I continued, "The good news is that your body is the best pharmacy ever. Once we start to get a handle on your anxiety, your body will produce its own 'sleep juice' like crazy and you will sleep normally. Sleep is almost like a positive side effect of your calm brain."

"I hope you're right. The only thing that works is falling asleep when I'm in front of the TV, but then I get up and go to bed and I'm up again. I know we're not supposed to fall asleep to the TV. It's really a vicious cycle," she said.

I encouraged her, "Take the sleep you can get for now. TV works because it shifts your brain waves closer to the sleep state. I used to joke that the PM in Tylenol pm stood for Perry Mason. If you have a television in your bedroom, you can use that until your body is sleeping naturally. We will help you understand your sleep cycles as well. Knowledge is power."

## Anxiety User Manual: It's Okay to Fall Asleep to the TV

If you're struggling with anxiety, you are most likely having difficulty falling asleep or staying asleep. Remember that high anxiety levels are akin to running from a lion. If your brain thinks you are running from a lion, proverbial lion or not, sleep is out of the question. Once again, your body is doing the right thing. Sleep is not a good idea when imminent danger is present. Sleep is the result of an unpreoccupied and relaxed brain.

I find my patients stress *a lot* about sleep at first, as did I. There is a great deal of pressure around getting "enough" sleep. Did you know that sleeping six to eight hours a night only came into being during the Industrial Age? It is not how we are designed. If you go back in time before the Industrial Age and when the sun set, people ate, maybe did some stargazing, played some music, and went to sleep. Usually for about four hours. They would wake up, and believe it or not, that's when a lot of babies were conceived. Nothing to do, it's dark, let's have sex. Then back to sleep for a couple of hours and wake up with the sun. In much of Europe, an afternoon nap is part of the culture; siestas are good. Getting six to eight hours of contiguous sleep is a construct perpetuated by capitalism and big pharma.

I do, however, understand on a core level how nice it feels to get a good night's sleep and I do not undervalue it. Understanding how your brain and sleep cycles work will help you to relax and catch some z's. It may take some practice, but it will come.

The brain waves I will discuss here are beta, alpha, theta, and delta. When you are wide awake, be it from life, work, or anxiety you're experiencing beta waves (13–40 Hz). These are high frequency, low amplitude waves, meaning fast and short. They barely look like waves—more like a pen moving up and down quickly and close together, across one line on a page of paper with barely any space between the up and down movement.

Alpha (8–13 Hz) has bigger, more relaxed waves than beta. I mentioned earlier that your brain naturally goes into this wave when you are watching television and alpha waves are present during hypnosis.

Did you ever pass your freeway exit without realizing it? Or head home when you meant to go somewhere else? You were on automatic and not focused on the task at hand. Your mind was drifting. This is the result of alpha waves.

Theta (10–12 Hz) is a deep meditative state, which can also be achieved with hypnosis. It is looser and bigger than alpha waves but smaller than delta waves.

Delta (1–4 Hz), which is your sleeping state, is low frequency and high amplitude, meaning slow and tall. As if you took your pen and drew big sprawling, arches in a flowing line taking up the height of several lines on the page. So, the trick to sleep is slowing down those brain waves.

Here's another important thing to know: we cycle through five sleep stages of consciousness during sleep.

Stage One: Your muscles relax and stop moving, for the most part, maybe a twitch here or there and your eyes move slowly behind your lids. You might still have some awareness of what's going on around you and can be woken up easily by some type of disturbance. This stage starts with alpha and moves into theta.

Stage Two: Your body temperature drops, your breathing and heart rate regulate and your eye movement slows down a great deal or stops. Theta waves are the dominant ones in stage two, but your brain also alternates between theta and sleep spindles. Spindles (10–15 Hz) produce an infusion of calcium ions into the cortical pyramid cells and are responsible for synaptic plasticity and memory consolidation.

Stage Three: These brain waves are big and slow. During this stage it becomes harder to wake you up. It is deep sleep; your breathing is slow and your muscles are very relaxed. If someone were to force you awake you would feel disoriented. You're surfing high-amplitude delta waves.

Stage Four: You're still producing delta waves, but now you are out cold. Your body is repairing itself.

Stage Five: Also, known as rapid-eye movement (REM) sleep, is the dream state. The eyes are moving back and forth at a good clip, your breathing becomes shallow, your heart rate increases as does your blood pressure. Your body inhibits its ability to move so that it doesn't act out its dreams. This comes about an hour and a half into your sleep cycle.

These cycles repeat themselves several times throughout the night, bringing you in and out of consciousness, so as you cycle back into stage one, your bladder might wake you up. Just pee and get back into bed. Don't worry and think, "Oh great, now I'm up." That just moves you closer to the awake beta wave. If you don't freak yourself out with worry about going back to sleep, it will be easier to do so. Your body was supposed to wake up and go to the bathroom and it is happy and primed to go back to sleep. Your body is in the mood for sleep.

Let's discuss getting your body in the mood for sleep to begin with. What you want to develop is good sleep hygiene. Science tells us that a body in motion stays in motion. If you want your body to rest, you must slow down. Don't expect your wide-awake brain to go from sixty to zero.

Think about how we put kids to sleep. It's a routine. It's a ritual. Perhaps we start with a nice warm bath, our voice levels change to a soothing tone, then maybe a bedtime story and soothing cuddles. We don't bombard them with all the things they have to do tomorrow and remind them of what they did wrong today. We get them into a calm, quiet, relaxed state. We help them slow down their brain waves and forget about the day until they drift into sleep. Adults need the same kind of ritual.

I'd like to share some things that will help you shift your brain waves from beta to alpha.

Reading quiets your mind by immersing you in a different world and distracting you from your worries. You might want to avoid page-turners. I understand reading can be difficult when you're anxious, but it's worth a try to get your brain out of beta and in the mood for sleep.

I never understood why people are told not to fall asleep to television. It does emit light, but it lures your brain into an alpha state. Many people fall asleep in front of the television and then *get up* to go to bed, only to find themselves awake again. I can only speak for myself, but in my experience, watching TV in bed works. Nothing too exciting. A calm nature show, science documentaries, or my favorite, black-and-white television shows.

Let me be clear, I am not talking about your phone or your computer tablets which are held close to your face and emit a different type of light. They do not help with sleep. You can listen to them, but don't look into them.

Listening to a soothing program can be conducive to bringing your brain into an alpha state. There are apps with adult bedtime stories, guided meditations, or soothing sounds that will quiet the distraction of anxiety.

Some aromatherapy releases neurotransmitters in your brain that induce an alpha state, which is why it's relaxing. Start with lavender in your diffuser and have a second one that is programmed to start an hour or two later that contains sandalwood. As I mentioned earlier, put body-safe lavender on the bottom of your feet.

Soak in a tub or jacuzzi to release the tension from your body. A tense body is not an easy thing to make go to sleep.

Make yourself a soothing cup of chamomile tea, Sleepytime tea, or even an old-fashioned cup of warm milk.

These are effective ways to relax the body and prepare yourself to sleep well. What do these all have in common? They all involve your senses. *Come to your senses.* They will free you from your overly active mind especially when you combine them.

Take naps. Many people avoid naps, thinking they won't sleep later at night. The opposite is true. Naps teach your brain how to sleep, plus they can be deep and restorative.

If something is upsetting you in the hours before bedtime, get it out of your head by writing it down and giving it to the universe to fix. Getting it out of your system will help you not to ruminate. The same goes for something you'd like to remember to do tomorrow. Write it down and get it out of your head.

Another thing I love to do is challenge my patients *not* to sleep. If you can't sleep, stop trying to sleep. The biggest enemy of sleep is the worry about not sleeping. When given the opportunity to relax the brain will produce a neurotransmitter called melatonin. Melatonin is your sleep juice. Anxiety produces cortisol and adrenaline, the arch enemies of melatonin. They inhibit its production. When your brain becomes calm you will sleep.

If you struggle with insomnia, chances are, the hours before bedtime are being spent dreading not being able to fall asleep. This is the best way to ensure a night of tossing and turning. When you stop *trying* to sleep, you tend to fall asleep, and if you don't you've at least stopped producing neurotransmitters like cortisol and adrenalin which keep you awake. My grandmother used to say, "I'll sleep plenty when I'm dead." Enjoy all your waking hours as best you can.

You might want to throw this book against the wall right now, but please don't. What I want you to understand is that your ticket dreamland is brought on by the release of your fears and obsessions. Put your focus on the life lessons and perspectives I am sharing with you throughout this book. Sleep will be the result of a quiet, peaceful, content mind. By now, some of the chapters are getting you there already. The following toolkit will help you fall asleep and these modalities can also help you go back to sleep if you have woken up in the middle of the night.

## Build Your Toolkit

Get your user manual.

1. Create a recipe for your sleep hygiene—that is, a list of relaxing behaviors. Make sure the items you choose include all five senses. You may have tried every one of the things I've mentioned but try putting several of them to use at the same time. There's strength in numbers.
2. Write down the basic bullet points of your current activity/ behavior that unfolds during the last hour before you usually go to sleep. Highlight the items that help you wind down.
3. Replace the bullet points of your activity that keep your brain awake with the behavior you listed in your recipe from exercise number one.
4. Be patient with this new practice. If you haven't slept well in ages, a few more weeks won't matter. It'll work better than what you are doing now. Get in the habit of developing and practicing your good sleep hygiene routine. Dim the lights and set the mood for sleep. Then give your body a chance to catch up to your new methods.

I've made a quick list of things to consider putting in your sleep recipe.

Warm bath or jacuzzi
Tea or warm milk
Aromatherapy
Dim lights
Massage tools
Slow stretching
Television
Sleep or meditation apps
Bedtime story apps
Reading
Gratitude lists

Get worries out of your head by journaling and giving them to your higher power.

Here are some items *not* to include in your sleep hygiene:

Don't spend hours worrying that you won't sleep.
Don't think about to-do lists.
Don't think about what you should have done differently.
Don't go over conversations that you have had or will have.
Don't do shoulda, woulda, coulda.
Don't engage in activating entertainment or behavior.
Don't consume caffeine after noon.

~

# CHAPTER TWENTY-SEVEN

# The Old Dope Peddler

Allow me to digress chronologically to my stay at the hospital after I had my heart attack.

As I sat bleary-eyed in the bed, a bearded figure appeared at my door. No white coat, no scrubs, no one who looked familiar, just a guy wearing a suit and tie. He approached my bedside with an outstretched arm, "Hi there, you must be Laura. I'm Dr. Goldstein."

I reached to return the greeting in confusion, "Hi."

He went on, "I'm a psychiatrist and I've been assigned to you by the hospital. The hope is we can hit it off by starting a session or two while you're here, and then we could continue our sessions at my office once you have been discharged."

Still out of it, I nodded.

"How does that sound?" He asked with the exuberance of having offered me a trip to Europe.

"Uh . . . okay. I guess." It felt like I had no choice in the matter.

"Okay then!" he shot back in an even cheerier tone. "Why don't I come by tomorrow at 2 p.m.? Would that work for you?"

*Like my dance card is full.* "Uh . . . I'm pretty sure I'll be here." I mustered a lips-closed thankful smile.

"See you tomorrow," accompanied the outgoing handshake, and off he went.

He returned the next day as he said and the session went well enough that I agreed to keep seeing him once out of the hospital, but really it was because he agreed to prescribe me anxiety meds and sleep meds.

His office was plain but nice. Black leather chair for him, black leather couch for me, and a fake ficus plant in the corner.

"Now that we've got a few sessions under our belt, let me be honest with you," he began.

*Wait, what?* Caution answers for me, "Ummmmmmm . . . okay."

"Your family has some real concerns about your addiction. It's one of my specialties, so how do you feel about addressing it?"

*I guess it doesn't matter how I feel, because here we are addressing it.*

I took a deep breath, "Okay. I'll admit I drink a little too much, however, pot is my drug of choice, and I won't smoke ever again, but I have had brutal migraines for the past ten years, and Vicodin is the only thing that helps. Plus, I hadn't slept until God created Ambien. So, thank God for Ambien." That part accompanied a nervous laugh on my end.

"It's great that you are prepared to give up the marijuana." He rubbed his hands together. "How about you lay off the booze, at least for now. I'll keep prescribing you the Klonipin, which should keep you nice and relaxed and I have no trouble giving you the Vicodin and Ambien. Migraines are brutal, and sleep is important. How does that sound?"

"I'm in." I agreed.

*Addiction specialist indeed.*

## Anxiety User Manual: Psychiatrists and Prescription Drugs

I want to state outright that I *am not* a doctor. The following information is based on my personal story and my experience in the field of therapy treating patients for anxiety, depression, and trauma.

There are some good and responsible psychiatrists out there, but sadly, in my experience, they are few and far between. It is heartbreaking when I see patients who have sought help for their anxiety or trauma, only to end up with a drug addiction on top of their already paralyzing fears. In short stacking one disease on top of another.

When I was an intern and getting my hours for licensure, a psychiatrist was brought in to present a lecture on prescription drugs to my cohort. He *actually* said, "There is no such thing as cross-addiction. You can prescribe alcoholic anxiety meds or sleeping pills without worrying they will become addicted." What?!

As I have said, always underneath anger is fear. Suffice it to say I was fuming! I did not have the nerve as a student to contradict him aloud, but it was like holding an inflated balloon underwater. I was bursting with contempt.

I have fought fruitless battles with some psychiatrists about the damage and danger that will ensue if they continue to stand in the way of titrating mutual patients off anxiety meds. Most anxiety meds are benzodiazepines. Benzos are not only addictive, but they also cause rebound anxiety. What does that mean? It means that the body will re-create the anxiety so it can get the meds. The addictive nature of these drugs tricks your body into wanting them. So, it goes like this. You're anxious. You take the pill. You calm down. Your body *craves* the substance and ramps your anxiety back up. You take another pill. Lather, rinse, repeat. Benzos are bad!

Here are some you might be familiar with: Valium, Ativan, Klonopin, Xanax, Lorazepam, and Alprazolam (most of the -ams and -pams). The list goes on and on. With friends like these, who needs enemies?

What I do support, when appropriate, is the use of antidepressants, or SSRIs (selective serotonin reuptake inhibitors). These pills allow your serotonin neurotransmitters to linger a little longer in your synapse, which allows your levels of joy to last a little longer. But they do not create serotonin. They do not create happiness. They extend the periods of the already present feel-good neurotransmitter to tamp down your depression long enough for you to do activities that help you create more serotonin and then you feel better. That said, they, too, can be disappointing and frustrating.

Many psychiatrists will see you for fifteen minutes, prescribe an SSRI, and let you know that if it doesn't work, they'll try another one in a couple of months, leading to a long ride of ups and downs that may or may not balance you out. This often leaves patients feeling like skeptical lab rats.

Full disclosure, since I started perimenopause, Prozac has helped me a great deal. So I am not against antidepressants, but it's vital to find a responsible psychiatrist who will listen to you, spend time with you, and prescribe the appropriate, helpful medication. There is genetic testing they can administer to get a better idea of what to prescribe to you on the first try. Your primary doctor can also prescribe SSRIs. In my experience most psychiatrists want to find ways to keep you on medication, not because they are bad people, but because they are trained to believe that is the solution. At my center, we focus on non-medicinal ways to self-soothe. Medication is a last resort.

Let's talk about sleep meds. No, no, and no! Again, there are exceptions to every rule, but in my experience, these are just another on-ramp to the highway of addiction. Here are some popular sleep meds to avoid: Lunesta, Ambien, and Sonata. They are all addictive. While sleep meds can work for short-term insomnia, they have the propensity to become addictive.

Our bodies are very efficient. If we introduce a chemical into our systems that produces sleep, our bodies stop making their own sleep juice. We don't make sleep juice, but sleep is a normal body function, and we have internal pharmacies and clocks that create healthy sleep patterns when given the opportunity.

It's not your body's inability to sleep that keeps you up. It is anxiety. Your head is not in your bed with you; it is fretting about the past or the future. When your anxiety returns to normal levels you will sleep the sleep of angels once again. I promise.

Warning! *Do not* just jump off *any* of your medication cold turkey. That can be dangerous. Make sure your doctor is on the same page if you wish to try new things and begin titrating off of your medication. Again, I am not a doctor; the methods I have shared with you in previous chapters are based on my own life experience and my expertise as a therapist.

Please remember that your anxiety is your alert system. Masking it doesn't change what is upsetting you. If a smoke alarm goes off, you can yank out the batteries so the noise stops bothering you, but you must still put out the fire. Drugs do not fix the problem, worse, they add to it.

## Building Your Toolkit

If you are taking medication and it is not helping or it is making things worse:

1. Share with your doctor that you are having trouble.
2. Consult with them about slowly coming off your meds.
3. If your psychiatrist is against taking you off medication, consider speaking to your doctor instead, or switching to a psychiatrist that thinks more broadly.
4. Look for a neurofeedback practitioner in your area, www.eeginfo. com. They can help you before you begin titration, during and after to make the transition easier and more effective.
5. Go back to chapters 22–26 and practice the techniques that will get you out of your head and into your body in the true moment.
6. Make a conscious decision to ditch the "quick fix" approach. Changing your brain will take some time, so be patient with yourself and be proud that you are taking the time to address your problems rather than masking them.

# CHAPTER TWENTY-EIGHT

~

# A Big Decision

The session ended and I wished my patient an easy weekend. My Director of Admissions was hanging around the door to her office in anticipation. She raised her head and eyebrows beckoning me her way.

"Pray tell, what's up?" I mused.

"It's bad news up front, but good news in the long run," she snickered.

"Okaaaaay," I said, as she jumped into the details.

"The office across the hall is opening up. I think we need to snatch it up," she waited.

I bit my lip. "How big is it?"

"I'm not sure." She went on, "The thing is, it looks like we are getting more and more calls as COVID is setting in. It seems like this ordeal is going to last for a while and we need to create the space, even if it is more expensive in the short term."

"Yeah, it ain't going anywhere quick. I'm glad we can stay open." My eyebrows furrowed in thought. "We do need to keep distance between people in groups, that's getting tougher to do in this space.

"That's what I was thinking," she said.

We went across the hall and asked the current tenants if we could look around. It was a big space, at least four thousand square feet. Our wheels turned as we wandered through the space. Thanking the tenants, we went back across the hall.

"Your opinion is important," I said to her. "Do you think we will get big enough to sustain the extra space after COVID is over?"

"Definitely. We are on the map and the calls are increasing every week." She was confident.

It was a big decision. I needed to think about it and speak with the rest of my board of directors. Not an actual board of directors, but that's what I call the people in my life that I go to when it comes time for big decision-making. My admissions director knew what the clinic needed, but she wouldn't be the one to help me crunch the numbers.

I asked my stepfather, who took care of billing at the clinic to go to dinner with me.

"That's a lot of space and overhead to take on," he said. "But based on the potential, I could see it working. Here's what I suggest. The need for office space is dwindling rapidly. See if your landlord will give you a break on the price per square foot."

"Great idea." My stomach was doing jumping jacks.

My mother added her two cents, "I think it would be fabulous!" I could always count on her to be a cheerleader when it came to new endeavors. She raised her glass, "Let's make a toast."

"It's a little early for that," I said. "I need to check out some more things." We raised our glasses anyway.

The next morning I called my brother. "It seems like a lot. What's your big picture? Do you really want to expand? Do you want to be like Barnes and Noble, or do you want to run a quaint bookstore in Maine?"

I appreciated the analogy. "Well, I have been asked to open other locations, but I know I don't want to do that. I need to maintain a certain amount of quality and service that would be hard to duplicate. Plus, I don't want to be all over the place and feel spread thin. So, I wouldn't go beyond this one facility." I thought of the pressure for a moment.

"I do want to provide as much help as I can for the community during COVID, not to mention, if it works, it could increase my bottom line substantially."

"If you think you can pull off and still enjoy your life, then I say go for it." Getting his support always made me feel better.

As I hung up the phone, my husband chimed in. "You have never made a move that hasn't worked for you when it comes to the Missing

Peace. Trust your gut. I support you on this. I'll do some of the build-out, and we can make it look just as cool as the rest of the space. I think it's exciting. I'm in 100 percent."

"Really?" I asked.

"This was just a matter of time. I knew you would have that whole floor eventually; COVID just put in on the fast track." He rubbed my shoulders.

I put my hand on his. "That's true. You really are the best. I love you."

The phone rang and it was my cousin, I put it on speaker. When I ran it by him, he said, "Now you'll have room to treat the whole family." We laughed. I can always count on him to make me laugh no matter how serious the topic.

In my head I could hear my father laugh, too. Even though he wasn't on this earth anymore, I could always check in with him and know in my heart what he would say.

"Blacky, if anyone can do it, it's you." He will always be on my board of directors.

That left my aunt, who would give me the conservative opinion; my sponsor, who helped me keep my motivations clean; and my sister, who, because we spent the first eighteen years together in the same room, sometimes knows me better than I know myself.

My intuition was saying yes, and my board agreed that it was the right move. The landlord gave me a break on the price and extended my current lease for another three years at the same price. Thank you, Universe! All the signs were there, the Missing Peace was about to expand! My board was right. It turned out beautifully, and the patients loved it, too.

## Anxiety User Manual: Appoint Your Board of Directors

My cousin once told me that people were like ice cube trays. No matter how carefully you place an ice cube tray in the freezer to be level, there will always be some cubes that come out shallower and some that overflow. People are the same. They are full of knowledge in some areas and less than helpful in other subjects. In other words, to acquire a full tray on every topic, I need a variety of people I trust to address different aspects of my life. It is impossible to have all your needs met by one person.

Couples can fall into this trap. They want their partners to fill every aspect of their lives, leaving them inevitably to fall short and disappoint one another. One person cannot be everything to you, because no one is everything. Your spouse should be someone you share your life with, but not your only source of support.

My friends meet different needs for me as well. I can vacation with some of my friends, but not all are good travel companions. I'd much rather try a new restaurant with one of my foodie friends, than a friend who is a vegan, unless it's a vegan restaurant and then bam, my choice changes. I wouldn't trust every person's entertainment choice, but some people in my life know my taste exactly. When those people suggest a show, I know I'm going to watch it and love it.

My moods require a variety of people as well. If I need a sympathetic ear and a shoulder to cry on my sister or brother would be a good call. But, if I am taking myself too seriously, my cousin who has a knack for finding humor in the darkest of situations is the perfect choice. I call a fellow Dodger fan if I want to geek out about the World Series. If my emotional sobriety feels threatened, I reach out to my sponsor. You get the idea.

By the same token, it is also important to know who *not* to call. If you suffer from anxiety, you probably have people in your life who increase your discomfort. When you're emotionally compromised, avoid these folks. Perhaps they mean well and want to help, but they only add to your worry and amp up your anxiety. You do not owe it to anyone to be included in your difficulties. You owe it to yourself to surround yourself with the helpers in your life, not the chaos creators and fire stokers. If you have people in your life who are toxic, it is okay to limit your time with them, or even separate yourself from them completely.

## Build Your Toolkit

It is helpful to have a go-to list of people in your life whose opinions you trust on different subjects. Get your user manual.

1. Make a Board of Directors page and earmark it for future use.
2. Write down your emergency contact person.
3. Write the name of your funniest friend.
4. Write the name of a friend who can give you good business advice.
5. Who is your most spontaneous friend, the person you can call at a moment's notice and go on an adventure with? Put them on the list.
6. Write down the person's name that will give you their honest opinion and not cosign your bullshit?
7. Who has known you longest? Is it the same person who knows you best? Put them on the list as well.
8. Is there someone who has passed on who always gave you sage advice? Include them too. You can always hear their thoughts in your own head.
9. Now make an Anti-Board of Directors page.
10. Write the name of someone who increases your anxiety.
11. Who are the doomsday predictors? Put them on the list.
12. Who are the miserable who love company? Put them on the list and perhaps consider allowing yourself to separate from them.

# PART III

~

# Re-Create Your Life

In part III the focus shifts back to the individual reading this book. It is about life beyond anxiety. It's time to find out what makes you happy on a personal level, both inside and out, so that you make every single day of your life hold moments of contentment and connection. Explore what motivates you and how you can change the possibilities of your destiny through the magic of spirituality and the quantum field.

# CHAPTER TWENTY-NINE

~

# Creating Our Dreamhouse

"What are your must-haves?" I asked my husband.

He thought for a moment before replying, "I want a three-car garage, a room to make my model trains, an office, and an extra tool room. What are yours?"

I did not need to think about it. I knew. "A pool, a view, a fireplace in the bedroom, a guest room, and an artist's den." Making a total checklist of ten must-haves.

"Sounds like a plan," he said. Then he looked up toward the ceiling, "Make it so." That was his way of making a request to the universe.

It was a tall order; we were nowhere near the economic status to afford such a place, but there was no rush. But if we're gonna dream, why not dream big? I knew the house would present itself when the time was right. I had a habit of looking in the Sunday paper at properties. As time went on, I found myself leaning toward Ventura, so I subscribed to a paper that showed homes in that county as well.

Five years later, during my weekend ritual of house perusing, I found a house that ticked all the boxes. The pictures weren't great, but we decided to go take a look. I called the real estate agent attached to the home and made an appointment for that morning and we headed over.

The house had a long driveway that led to the three-car garage, *check one*, at the top, the driveway surrounded a large island boasting a majestic pine tree, trimmed by fresh lavender bushes, roses, and wild-flowers. Gorgeous. We walked the atrium path adorned with camellias and ferns, through the dated eighties-style front door. It opened to a gob-smacking view. *Check two.* The carpet was off-white, wrinkled, and old. Easily removed. My mind saw hardwood floors. While the front of the house faced the breadth of the sprawling driveway, the entire back of the house was lined with glass windows and doors revealing three hundred degrees of trees and farmland, and *oh yes*, the pool in the back yard! *Three down, seven to go.*

My husband headed straight for the garage. "Oh my God!" He yelled. It had an attached tool room. *Check four.* There was no fire-place in the primary, *but* there was a huge family room downstairs that poured onto the pool area and guess what it had? YES! A brick fireplace! My creative juices were drooling. Downstairs there were two more rooms and a bathroom. *In a couple of years, we could convert one of the rooms and the bathroom into a terrific primary bathroom/closet making a killer primary suite. What to do with the other room?*

"Sweetie! I think I found your train room!" I called out.

By converting the downstairs, the bedrooms upstairs would become an office, a guest room, and the primary bedroom could be my artist's den. *Bingo!* The must-have list was fulfilled. *This was our house.*

In reality, getting a loan of this amount was a stretch, but I felt it in my gut and the universe would show the way. I knew it was meant to be. I called the agent who helped us buy our current home. He was skeptical that we would get it, being that it had only been on the market one day. I was not worried. This was the one. The loan officer said we could be preapproved with a high-interest bank statement loan. My brain said no and my intuition said yes. We put in a full-price offer, and I bought area rugs for the living room and the primary room the next day. Everyone thought I was crazy, but my soul brimmed with excitement.

We were met with hurdle upon hurdle. They had a cash offer. It fell through. They wouldn't enter into a contract until our house was in es-crow. Three days later, our house was sold. The new owner would have to wait for us to close. No problem. The house was older, so inspection might present several red flags. They were all green; it was outdated but kept up impeccably. No matter what issues arose, my faith was unwavering. Every night in bed I gazed starry-eyed at the ceiling, planning, decorating, manifesting, and smiling.

Much to the surprise of our loan officer, the funds were approved early. The interest rate was insane, and the mortgage payment was high, but I have learned the universe will provide abundance when I come from abundance. And it has. We saw the house for the first time on September 24. We took possession seven and half weeks later on November 15. Thank you, Universe.

## My Re-Creation Manual: Quantum Physics? Or Beyond?

As you escape the grip of anxiety, a new you will emerge. In the rooms of Alcoholics Anonymous I began to understand the phrase "life beyond your wildest dreams" on a visceral level. The connection to a higher power changed my life, and I watched as it transformed the lives of the people around me who had spiritual connections. My life has grown exponentially, and so my trust in a higher power grew. I kept leaping and flying.

In hindsight I accessed it my whole life without being consciously aware of it. I remember my neighbor got a beige Toyota Celica when I was fourteen, and I prayed that I would get one someday. In my twenties, I bought a beater car for $500 with the door kicked in, but it worked, and I needed a car. About three months into owning it, I realized it was a beige Toyota Celica. I guess when I prayed for it, I forgot to mention the condition it should be in! So now I am more specific, hence my must-have list for my house. I have watched my patients create their dreams by trusting the universe and developing a connection to their intuition and abundance.

My only frustration has been the longing to comprehend how this amazing force of nature works. Quantum physics is as close to an explanation as I can get. In chapter 24 I discussed working with your energy and changing your frequency. Quantum field theory explores the connection and oneness between all subatomic particles. Imagine a field of energy that holds *every possibility and outcome there is now* and *every outcome that can be*. That is the quantum field.

Objects which are part of a galaxy millions of light years away are also a part of us. We are one. This is where science and Eastern philosophy overlap. The difference is science has found indications that suggest this oneness and has spent decades in labs and thousands of dollars trying to find empirical evidence of its "proof." Whereas Eastern philosophy knows that it is true and believes that it's a mystery is not for us to solve, but merely to experience.

Science shares that everything in this universe is made of energy. Einstein's theory of relativity, E=MC² states that energy is equal to mass times the speed of light squared at which it travels. Matter is the measurement of mass. He also explained that matter that is detected by our five senses and is energy that moves slowly enough for us to perceive it. For example, a chair is made up of matter that is moving so slowly that to humans it appears stationary and permanent. The chair is energy and is connected to energy throughout the universe. We are also one with the universe. The universe, the chair, and you are part of one living entity. But the chair, just like you, does not contain the same *frequency* as everything else, only some things.

When two entities have the *same frequency*, in the quantum field, this phenomenon is described as quantum entanglement with coherence; two things that occupy separate locations but contain the same frequency. Therefore, the frequencies that we emanate can connect with like frequencies in different planes of spacetime and already hold the *possibility* of being one.

Our brains are made up of electromagnetic energy and have their own quantum field. This means the things you think and feel send energy waves with specific frequencies into the universe. They will connect with matching frequencies in the universe.

The electricity in our brains can be measured by an EEG, which I discussed in chapter 23. We can also measure the brain's magnetic force with an MEG (magnetoencephalogram). Together they create the EMF (electromagnetic field), which gives us access to the physical and tangible world around us via our five senses.

On the other hand, the quantum field in our brain is associated with the nontangible, such as consciousness. We know our consciousness exists, but we have yet to fully understand it or account for how it works.

Our thoughts and feelings generate our reality. When we feel hate inside, we attract cruel people and unpleasant encounters. If we feel compassion inside, we attract caring people and pleasant situations. Is the glass half-empty or half-full? Or is it half water and half air? It is what you think and feel. When your thoughts contain fear, your body feels anxiety, causing you to limit the experiences in your life. The people you meet and the places you encounter will diminish based on your fearful frequency. The opposite is also true. When your thoughts contain abundance and your feelings generate joy and gratitude, your life grows, and your experiences become richer.

I will expand on what happens when I have come from a fear-driven place to create my "dreams" in the next chapter. Fear-driven manifestations don't generate the best outcomes. There is a way to tell the difference.

It is important to keep in mind that the universe is not your genie. It is a living entity. It has access to the bigger picture, where we do not. As much as I wanted my father to live, that was not in the stars. His soul had his connection with the universe and they had a plan that did not involve me. When the universe says "no," I trust that too.

But we don't have to understand the magic of the universe to experience its bounty. Imagine how difficult it would be for a goldfish to understand that we go to Petco and buy tetra flakes. If it needed hard evidence of why the food existed and how it came to be it would sit at the bottom of the tank fretting and starving. On the other fin, if it swims around, eats the food, and looks at the castle without needing to understand it all, life is abundant and easy.

Some quantum physicists proffer the idea that all possibilities are available in the quantum field; it is just a matter of thinking and feeling them to generate such outcomes. Some quantum physicists do not believe this is possible.

The one thing I know for sure is that science is always expanding its knowledge base. We still don't have all the answers, at least not in the concrete terms required by some scientists. The mystery of how the universe operates is alive and growing. The boundaries of scientific knowledge are elusive. I have learned that I don't have to understand how manifesting works, I only have to trust that it does. The ideas are up to me. The how is up to the universe. When I come from a good place, it turns out even better than my original wish. Life beyond my wildest dreams.

I will never stop searching for the *how* completely. I believe we are created with a desire to search for knowledge and understanding of the world around us. But I will continue to trust whatever *it* is and create a beautiful life for myself. So, dream big and see what happens.

## Build Your Toolkit

You've got your anxiety user manual. Always keep your anxiety user manual close. It has taken me years of practice and repetition to master my anxiety. Keep your practice growing. However, the time has come to expand on your journey. You are going to manifest life beyond your anxiety.

1. Get a fresh, new, blank book.
2. Name it "My Re-Creation Manual."
3. Write an entry to yourself that from this day forward you promise to be willing, open, and teachable in creating the life you always wanted. Be unwavering! Omit any fearful and doubtful thoughts from your writing.
4. Make a short list of your desires. Then imagine the thoughts and feelings you will send out to the universe that would generate the outcome you'd like. For example,
   Thought: I want a job that gives me the freedom to be with my kids, relieves my stress, and supports our lives easily.
   Feelings: Joy, gratitude, relief, excitement.
5. Now write it on a piece of paper and stick it to your wall. Every day, take a minute or two to imagine your scenario. You don't have to know what the job will be or how it will happen. That is up to the universe.
6. Now feel those feelings that you listed, from your head down to your toes, and picture the energy of those feelings emanating from you into the universe. Then wait. It will come.

# CHAPTER THIRTY

~

# Fear-Based Manifesting

Authors today are told that if they don't have a platform with millions of followers no agent or publisher will take them on. The only other way to gain traction with your book is to have an influencer with a large following either write your foreword, or at the very least, give you a personal quote about the book, known as a blurb for your book cover. Fear struck my heart. I had been building my platform, but I was nowhere near an impressive count. Where could I find an influencer?

As adrenaline and cortisol filled my body, a memory appeared in my head. My mother and stepfather have touted for years that they are the ones who encouraged a now leading motivational speaker to write his first book. *Maybe they could ask him to give me a blurb?*

When I asked my stepfather, he said they hadn't spoken for years, but perhaps he could reach out to his friend who had been the original publisher for the book.

"Great!" I said, hoping to quiet the panic in my body, but I couldn't just let it be. I searched the internet and found out the author would soon be doing a show in Los Angeles. I told my stepdad to ask his publisher friend if we could say hello to the author before the show. His friend said to mention her name at the door, and we would be granted access to the green room. I did not trust it. I wanted something more solid. My fear told me that we would need more than "She said we could" to gain entrance to the green room at the Shrine Auditorium. *I need this!* The prospect of getting a world-renowned author/speaker to endorse my book would spark an agent's interest like dynamite blasting into a hill hiding priceless gems.

The week before the event, I could feel myself getting antsier. A gaping pit in my stomach churned every time the encounter entered my mind. The imagery I was creating was not good. *What if he says no? We are never going to get back there.* As the date neared closer my worries about the meeting spiked and I became even more unsure. Fearing I would never speak to him again after this event, I pre-wrote some blurbs for him to sign at the very least.

Finally, the day came, the show started at 7 p.m., but the doors opened at 5:30. I had an hour and a half to accomplish my mission. My stepfather and I went directly to security and told them the publisher said we could go to the green room.

"No visitors without a wristband," he said firmly.

My inner struggle commenced and my desperation forced panic through my body. *I've got to do this! The book depends on it.* I motioned to my stepdad to follow me. I found one of the curtains leading backstage. It was blocked by guards.

"Hi there," I explained how and why should be allowed into the green room.

"Go to will call and see if they can help you," the guard said.

On the way to will call, my stepdad pointed to the Lost and Found table, and said, "Maybe they can help."

One of the two girls at the table said, "Oh, if you know him personally, just go around back to the loading docks. That's how you get backstage."

My ears perked up.

The second girl's face had a "you should not have told them that" look, as she said, "I think they should go to will call."

"Thanks so much," I said smiling. *Thank you indeed. The heck with will call; we are heading to the alley.* I took my stepfather by the hand and dragged him outside. The alley was barricaded by an armed policeman and two security men, who asked if we were on the guest list. I gave him the name of the publisher.

Without realizing it the guard held the list so far in front of himself, it gave me the chance to read some of the names. "Sorry, I don't see her on the list," he said as his arms fell behind him, hiding the list away.

*Am I really going to do this? I am.* I regurgitated a name I saw on the list.

"How about John Flint?"

He looked again, "John Flint. There it is."

*I can't believe that fucking worked. I am Obi-Wan Kenobi. The force is with us! Thank you, Universe!*

We were so close. My heart pounded like I was riding the final loop on Space Mountain. I could see the green room light glowing through the doorway guarded by a security guy next to the closed door.

"We are on the guest list," I said, and I reached for the doorknob before he could respond.

As the door opened, I found myself in a tiny three-by-six room, one foot away from the author who was privately meditating in a small wooden chair. His eyes popped open in surprise. I halted in my steps and jerked to the left, so as not to end up on the poor man's lap. I wasn't sure who was more shocked, him or me.

He politely rose from his chair and after a confused moment, he hugged my stepdad.

My stepdad inquired, "Are you in town for long? We'd love to take you to dinner."

But before the author could respond the door was thrown open by a woman who was, suffice it say, very agitated, "You people should not be in here!"

My stepdad jumped, "Sorry for the confusion; Caroline said we could come down here."

The author, anxious to get back to his meditation, said, "Well I'm leaving tomorrow, do you have a card? Maybe I can be in touch."

*This does not feel right.* It felt awful. But I was possessed by desperation. I needed to make this happen. "I have heard so much about you, and I run an anxiety center. I notice you don't often write forewords . . ."

"I do," he interrupted, "but I like to read the book first."

"I've brought you some sample chapters and some blurbs, if . . ." I was interrupted by a tall pony-tailed woman, "I'm sorry," she yelled, "You two need to get out of here now!"

*This is a trainwreck.* I ignored her and handed him the chapters.

"You need to leave now!" she continued her shouting as we were escorted out of the tiny room.

At the same time, the guard from the lobby was standing there seething. "You knew you were not supposed to be down here." He said, through clenched teeth. As he escorted us out of the venue, my mother, who had no idea what had happened, was hysterical.

The melodrama started as my mother pleaded with the security guard. "Why are you doing this to me? I can't walk! I don't understand this. What's wrong with you people?"

It was quite a scene in the aisles of the Shrine Auditorium that night. Over the years, many people have been thrown out of many concerts, but the shocked faces of the guru-following, peace-seeking audience did not expect to see this tonight.

I got my chapters to the author, but I was not feeling like a great manifester. I felt desperate and dirty. At the very least, I was being thrown out of a theater, but at the very worst, I had sullied my chances with this author, and perhaps even tainted the relationship between him and my stepfather.

*What has happened? I got past every obstacle with sheer will. With all my might I endeavored to approach the Universe with my fear of failing frequently. It gladly complied. What have I done?*

As I drove us home, the silence was broken by my mother, "Laura, I need chocolate."

The author still hasn't replied. Not a surprise.

## Re-Creation Manual: Worry Is Praying for What You Don't Want

We have the power to manifest. But the energy and frequency from which we manifest will predict the outcome. In the story I just shared, I came from panic and fear. I was sending the universe vibrations of lack and discord and therefore that is what I received. It met me exactly where I was. No judgment, simply an equal response to my energy and thoughts. The quantum field meets our electromagnetic energy to a tee because the thoughts we are thinking and feeling are one with the results we ultimately achieve.

Using my stories as an example, when I got fired, I didn't take my next step out of fear. I paused, reached out to my board of directors, and came from a place of intuition and excitement that produced my treatment center. With our house, I did not connect with the energies of the skeptical real-estate agent, or the difficult sellers. I manifested our house with confidence and an inner knowing that it was meant to be. If I had simply asked my stepfather to get in touch with the author and then trusted it would happen, the results would have been different. But I gave into my fear-based thinking. I bought into the idea that I had to get this influencer or my book would never get published. My anxiety was predicting doom.

This incident left me in a funk for a week or two. Then I got off my pity pot and used my tools. First, I forgave myself for being human and having normal fear-based thinking. Then I summoned compassion for giving into my Wounded Child and letting her run the show. I turned to my higher power and put my care back into its hands, reminding myself of the love and trust I have in the universe. I sent a mental prayer to this author and apologized for invading his space and breaking his meditation before his show. I hope he felt it.

Once I let go of the fear, and realigned my frequency with success, the quantum field responded. Six weeks later, I had an agent and a publishing deal. I did not need an influencer or a platform, just faith that the quantum field exists, and this book was meant to get published no matter what.

## Build Your Toolkit

You are going to make a "Universe Box."

1. Find a container of any shape or size you'd like. You can buy one, find one around your house, or even use a shoe box.
2. You can decorate it if you'd like, or you can leave it just the way it is.
3. Find a scrap of paper and write down something that worries you.
4. Now fold it up and put it into your Universe Box.

5. Transform the feelings of worry you were sending to the universe by writing down the feelings you would experience if it came out the way you wanted it to. If those negative feelings return, realign yourself with the good feelings you wrote down.

6. Keep this box, or one like it forever. Each time you worry, give it to the universe and trust the results.

# CHAPTER THIRTY-ONE

~

# My Happy Place

Where am I? The typical discomfort of morning angst awakened me. Knowing that I had just awoken from the stage of sleep in which I process my stressors helped my disorientation dissipate quickly, and my anxiety settled down. I was in a hotel room in Hawaii. My eyes closed again, and I invited them to take their sweet time to reopen. There was no rush. There was never a rush in Hawaii.

Being the early riser of my group made Kona coffee my morning companion. Ahhhh, and it was only twenty feet from my bed. Draping the white waffle robe around my freshly tanned body, I parted the curtains and basked in the island's beauty gleaming through my window. Varying colors of green and blue melted across the view like sweet honey. The moment was perfect. I couldn't think of a better way to start my day.

The air conditioning was great for a good night's sleep, but the chill in the room didn't match my morning bliss. A dip in the jacuzzi would be just the ticket. I double-checked for my room key as the door closed behind me. It took a few minutes to dismiss my inner thoughts. As I made a mindful effort to connect with the moment, the song of tropical birds scoring my saunter to the pool area came alive. I took a sip of my coffee and warmed my dry throat as I tuned in. *Coffee, sunshine, blue sky, ocean waves—this is the good life.* I reached for the phone in my pocket to check in with the office, but I stopped myself. No multitasking. Anything that needed my attention could wait. I would start the day on my terms. *I wish I could do this at home.*

Sliding into the jacuzzi unfolded my muscles from nighttime clenching. I found my thoughts trying to tug me out of the moment and drift to issues at work, so, I closed my eyes and listened to the relaxed rhythm of my breathing, and then I slipped into deep meditation. During the meditation a thought crossed my mind that deserved further entertaining. *Why don't I do this at home? The apartment building I live in has a jacuzzi.* I put a pin in it and drifted off again.

Back in the room, I set the stage for morning video calls. I moved the comfy chair to the desk and positioned myself to take in the view. My sessions went well. How could they not on a day like today? I made sure to schedule a break for lunch at my favorite restaurant with enough time to drive by the waterfall and take a dip. Whenever my thoughts drifted to problems or issues that were not in the car with me, I brought myself back to the present moment. Energy restored, I returned to the hotel, and did my afternoon sessions.

Around 5:30 my phone rang. It was my cousin.

"Aloha," I said.

"Aloha," he replied. "Have you finished healing the world?

I loved his sarcasm. "I am open for some fun."

He went on, "K. We are back from snorkeling. I think we are going to head to the pool and watch the sunset."

"I am so down for that. Meet you there," I said.

"Aloooohaaaa." He hung up.

Upon my return home from Hawaii, my little epiphany during my meditation resurfaced. I was making my second cup of morning coffee, and I decided to take it out to the jacuzzi. It became a part of my routine. I would start my day just like I did on vacation. The idea grew. I put a coffee machine in my upstairs bathroom, so I could get the first sip of java without going downstairs, just like at the hotel. I moved my office around to face the window and changed the décor to evoke the "islands zhuzh." I don't eat lunch at the office anymore. I head to a restaurant or park with some kind of rejuvenating ambiance. No more waiting for weekends or two weeks of vacation a year to enjoy my life. From that trip on, I made it a point to build joy into my day, no matter what.

## My Re-Creation Manual: Make Your Life a Vacation

Most of us have to work for a living. Whether it's in an office, a restaurant, or managing your home and kids, life tends to produce a lot of to-dos and many of us get so overwhelmed by them, we believe there is no time for recreation. All work and no play. Let's break down the meaning of the word recreate: Re-Create. Our playtime is meant to rejuvenate and revive us.

Have you ever said, "I can't wait to stop for gas!" I haven't. But I do it no matter what because the idea of pushing my car to a gas station or calling roadside service is not an ongoing viable option. Tragically, so many people run on empty. Not for a mile or two, but for years! Stress and exhaustion are playgrounds for anxiety and depression.

If you want to draw a life of abundance to yourself, you must bring positive fulfilling energy into your daily routine. The good news is that it's a lot more pleasurable than stopping for gas. There are more hours in the day than you think. I promise you, there is time for you to build joy into your life. I have helped hundreds of patients who were too busy to awaken to the idea that not only is there time for play, but the quality of their work has grown exponentially due to the fact they make time for recreation. This gives credence to the concept of working smarter, not harder.

One of my favorite stories involves a patient who was a busy, high-powered lawyer. He loved the beach and when his toes were in the sand, he felt relaxed and grounded.

He said, "I wish I could practice law on the beach in Cabo San Lucas."

I suggested he put a sand tray under his desk. No one else would know it was there, but his toes would feel like they were in Mexico. He did it! He loves it! Two other people in his firm did the same thing. It's little adjustments to your routine that will bring you happiness and fill you up.

One of my directors at the office does not like the feel of sand on her feet; she thought the idea was crazy. For her it was. As always, different things work for people. Not everyone wants a coffee machine twenty feet from their bed. I do. What do you like on vacation? Let's find a way to bring it into your daily life.

## Build Your Toolkit

Get your Re-Creation Manual.

1. What's the first(s) thing you do when you wake up in the morning if you are on vacation? Write it/them down.
2. Figure out a way to start your day that way and beginning tomorrow do it no matter what. If you need to get up a little earlier, do it. Fill your tank, before your day starts going.
3. Write what your favorite view is on vacation.
4. Make a point of incorporating some of those features into the space you occupy daily—be creative. Use pictures, plants, lights, any décor, or elements to remind you of that place. Make it more than just a screen saver.
5. Write down the sounds that make you feel happy on vacation.
6. Pick one of those sounds and have it near you during the day, either playing in the background or ready to play for a few minutes to recharge yourself.
7. Now write down anything else that pops into your mind that brings you pleasure or relaxation from your vacations. What gets you into that "vacation mindset"?
8. Create room for them wherever you can! Don't wait for a vacation to treat yourself to your favorite things.
9. Make a conscious decision to put things on the back burner that can wait, like enjoying your breakfast without answering a call or reading emails.

# CHAPTER THIRTY-TWO

~

# Romance Yourself

I couldn't believe how beautiful the Seine was. I mused at how many years it flowed through Paris amid revolution, Nazi occupation, *liberte*, tourists, and the company of countless artists from Monet to Rodin. The Seine remained ever present, stalwart, serene, and strong.

My husband and I went our separate ways after breakfast. He wanted a scooter day, and I wanted to be with myself. The wind breezed across all the right places on my neck and face as I meandered under the shade of the *Jardin de Tuileries*. I passed by a businessman in his suit, gesturing, speaking into his cellphone, and doing his part to make sure the world remained functional. I was glad that was not on my agenda today.

I hailed a cab and headed to *Montmartre*. The smell of diesel assaulted my senses as we drove through the crowded, bricked-back roads to the *Sacre Coeur* Church. It reminded me of Nob Hill. The taxi driver said, "Dix Euro, Madam." I gave him an extra two euros. "Merci et bon journee, Madam," he said hurrying from the car to open my door and let me out.

The steps of the church weren't steep, and I wandered up the path past several sandwich boards that listed hot dogs and fish and chips. *No way. I'm looking for crepes!* I found a small café. As I waited for my food, my mind traveled back through time, and played images of me sipping a café au lait and having a lively conversation with Gertrude Stein and Alice, while Hemingway drank too much Absinthe and started a fistfight with some guy in a beret. Gertrude barely noticed the brawl, because, well, that was just Ernie.

My fantasy was interrupted by a caricature artist who had convinced some poor tourist to stand uncomfortably, in the same position, for fifteen minutes, while he sketched a far-from-accurate cartoon of who they were. There must have been five artists within this twenty-by-twenty space. "Who weel be da lucky wone?" They shouted with French accents.

It seemed to me that twelve out of ten Parisiennes smoked. *That's how the women stay so skinny.* I declined a request for my caricature to be drawn, which must be done twice, in both French and English, to effectively have the artist move on. I ate my way through the perimeter of the crepe and arrived at the savory, creamy center. "Mmmm" ecstasy left my lips every few bites.

A group of college students clad in high-waisted jeans and backpacks filled the promenade. They followed a guide holding a light blue flag. I turned my head to avoid the cloud of cigarette smoke. I watched a croque monsieur and a hamburger being served to the table next to me. The woman eating the croque had very pretty hands with blue nail polish, and as she rubbed the back of her hamburger-eating boyfriend, I noticed a bizarre ring that was shaped like a snake and wrapped up, down, and around three of her fingers. *I am fully in the moment.* All my senses engaged, smell, sight, sound, touch, and taste. Heaven. I haven't thought about work in over a week. Travel was great for staying in the moment and shutting down my anxiety. Laura 1, anxiety 0.

My first trip to Paris had been fun, but my anxiety had distracted me, making it difficult to be in the moment long enough to enjoy it. I felt different this time. I benefited from a sense of serenity that came from becoming adept with my tools. My insides felt at peace while I people-watched. The clang of a passing tram overpowered the sounds of the crowds for a second. *I can't believe I am here in Paris working on a book.* I was jealous of myself. I sat, gently in awe of life. I bought a flower from a passing vendor. It was a well-deserved, romantic outing with me. After years of work, I enjoyed my own company. *I could sit here for hours.*

## Re-Create Your Life: The Arm around You Must Be Your Own

Ever since I was teenager and longing for a boyfriend to feel loved, my mother annoyed me with the saying, "When you can walk down the beach at sunset and the arm around you is your own, that is when you'll know the greatest love possible." Whitney Houston sang a song with those sentiments as well. It's true. But it is much easier said than done.

I am notorious for encouraging my patients to love themselves.

"But how?" is the usual response.

"Romance yourself," I say.

The idea is usually scoffed at. "Oh sure, like buy myself flowers? I'll feel so stupid. Buying myself flowers feels . . . kind of pathetic, don't you think?" They say.

Strangely, society portrays romance as something that only comes from someone else and not yourself. Why do so many of us feel silly treating ourselves to acts of love? Doing such things for yourself can be mistakenly associated with loneliness. A sad predicament implying that no one else is there to do it, so you have to do it for yourself. How backward.

In my experience, I wasn't able to have a meaningful relationship with another until I knew how to love myself. I was so grateful for any crumb that was thrown my way, I treated it like a feast. Then, as time went on, the mere crumb left me hungry and, yes, lonely. I was lonelier in bad relationships than I was when I was single. What made me settle for such empty relationships? It was the desperation to find love at any cost. It turns out, that was not the love I needed. I had to find it within myself first.

The truth is we all need different kinds of love. What works for some, doesn't work for others. The best way to learn how you like to be loved is to discover it for yourself. It is up to you to figure out what soothes you at the end of a long day. Your free time deserves a chance to be explored. Weekends and alone time are there to fill you up, not be spent wondering why no one is there with you. Even if you have a partner, it is still up to you to refill your tank. The odds of finding a like-minded partner go way up when you know your likes and dislikes before you meet. The best relationships are comprised of two individuals who know how to meet their own needs. The idea of having some-one else complete you is misguided and unhealthy.

Life begins outside of your comfort zone, so try different things. For example, I used to hate eating in restaurants or going to the movies alone, but now I love it! The best way to rediscover yourself is to be adventurous. That doesn't mean jumping out of a plane necessarily, it means thinking outside of your day-to-day routine. Indulge yourself in ways you would want a romantic partner to entice you. Take yourself to places you have never been before. Select outings for yourself that you haven't thought of trying on your own. Where would you want someone else to take you? Take yourself there! You can stay as long as you like or leave early. When you're on a date with yourself, you're the only one you need to please! You can go to any movie you want. You can visit any city you want. You can follow any artist you want. You can listen to any music you like. You might find new music to like! Try playing an instrument. Maybe it's not your gift, but maybe it is. Paint, sculpt, draw a bath, plant, ski, knit, golf, sing, dance, run, walk, cook, eat out, eat in, sleep late, get up early, read, laugh at videos, make a video, try it all! Use the full spectrum of life's pallet to create your life.

Don't expect to love everything but give yourself a chance to try anything. If you were courting someone else, you would keep trying different things to please them, and if you cared enough, you wouldn't stop until you found something that brought a smile to their face. Do that for yourself. Don't give up. Everybody likes something. It's your right to find out how to please yourself. Wouldn't it be great to bring a smile to your face? You don't need someone else to do that. You can walk down the beach at sunset and the arm around you can be your own.

## Build Your Toolkit

Get your Re-Creation Manual.

1. Write down five romantic gestures.
2. Write down five romantic restaurants you've always wanted to go to.
3. Write down five things you'd want your love relationship to say to you.

4. Write down five ways you would want to be greeted when you got home by a romantic partner.
5. Write down five things you'd like to receive as a gift from a romantic partner.
6. Write down five places you'd like to go with a romantic partner.
7. Do at least one thing from your list for yourself every week.
8. Start falling in love with yourself!

# CHAPTER THIRTY-THREE

~

# What Should I Be
# When I Grow Up?

The game of Trivial Pursuit was cut short with tears of laughter.

My brother wiped his eyes and pointed to me, "Why don't you ask Einstein over there?"

"Right?" I said doubling over, "Who knew I would be the one who ended up with a degree in science?"

"Definitely not me," my cousin chuckled. "I had you pegged for dead comic."

My mother broke the mood, "Well, I don't think that's funny."

"Come on, Ma, we're just kidding around." My sister said half-laughing, "Are you telling me that you thought Laura would end up as a therapist?"

"Well, no," said my mother, "But then who ended up being anything we expected? Except you." She pointed to my cousin.

My aunt chimed in, "That's true, I always said you'd be a musician. When I was pregnant with you, if music played, you'd start banging your fists," she said.

"Vat do you vant, it makes me heppy," my cousin said in a Yiddish accent.

My aunt pointed at him. "That's all that matters! Thank God it was keyboards, I couldn't have taken drums."

My brother commented, "I wouldn't want to do what any of you do. I like peace and quiet."

"That's probably why you moved so far away from family," my sister shot back.

We all laughed a little. Then the conversation became more introspective.

I spoke up, "I still can't believe I do what I do. If you had told me thirty years ago that I would be sober, happily married with no kids, and running an anxiety center, I would have thought you were drunker than I was."

"Ya, no kidding," said my brother.

I thought about what my cousin had said. He wasn't far off. Had I stayed in the entertainment field, I probably would be dead by now. It bred so much insecurity for me, the auditions, the pressure, waiting for callbacks. And being an agent was worse. I had to be completely stoned to get through the day.

My stepfather said, "Your job has to be aligned with your purpose and driving force. To be happy, your soul's purpose needs to be fulfilled, and most often we do that through work. Sometimes we don't discover it right away. For example, you were great at sales," he pointed to my sister, "but you weren't happy because you needed to be working with children. Then you became a doula and voila, you're happy."

"True dat," my sister went on. "Wish I had figured that shit out earlier."

As the evening went on, we took turns connecting the dots that led us each to our destiny. It had not been a linear process for any of us. Each of us seemed to take detour after detour collecting little pieces along the way that would eventually produce who we were today. Every side trip that seemed erroneous at the time was a vital part of creating a bigger picture.

## My Re-Creation Manual: Purpose and Driving Force

Some of us are blessed with the gift of knowing our driving force from the time we are born, but many of us are not. Or some of us think we knew only to find out later, that we did not.

How we spend each day and what we do during that time contributes greatly to how we feel inside. Therefore, it follows that it's important to choose your purpose/career following your passion to enjoy your everyday life. It helps to know what drives you. What is the particular brand of motivation that gets you out of bed with a bounce in your step? I'd like to define both purpose and driving force, as it relates to this chapter and its overall concepts.

### Driving Force: Your Soul's Calling; Your Passion

*Purpose: The Chief Role You Play in Your Day-to-Day Life*

Let's take a look at some driving forces as they correlate to some careers. There are many more, but here are a few examples.

Influence: You hold the power to guide people. People look to you for answers and you enjoy being a leader. Career: CEO, politician, religious leader, teacher, blogger

Recognition: You want to make your mark on the world. You want to create something that will be remembered or seen as someone who is revered. Career: inventor, architect, actor, writer

Service/Spirituality: You enjoy helping others; money can be involved but it doesn't have to be. Assisting others to achieve their needs makes you happy. Career: nurse, therapist, volunteer, parent

Harmony: You want peace and simplicity. You are a great team player but want to avoid any stress or big decision-making. Career: office worker, landscaper, librarian

Many of us identify with more than one of these categories, but identifying your primary driving force will help you select your purpose.

But here's the thing. I did not find my true purpose overnight. It was a series of events, all of which made me happy in the moment and led me unwittingly down the path I am on now. I just kept following my intuition, as crazy as it might have seemed. I just needed to keep taking the *next right-indicated step*. One step at a time. Since I have already told you much of my story, I will sum up my *next right-indicated steps* with more brevity.

I was unhappy in the entertainment field and almost drank myself to death, then I got sober. I followed my sponsor's direction to just be in the moment, and I went on a whimsical trip to Sedona. In Sedona I had a spiritual experience that, much to my surprise, sparked an intrigue in doing past life regressions (PLR), which gave my family a lot of laughs, but I knew what I had to do. PLR peaked my interest in becoming a hypnotherapist which somehow led to me the joyful craft of teaching meditation. At one of the facilities where I taught meditation, I learned neurofeedback leading me to open a neurofeedback practice. I loved doing it and I could make my own hours. The clients seem to come from nowhere, but they came.

One of my clients said, "I wish you were my real therapist."

I thought, *Why not?* Who cares if I'm forty-five? I finished my bachelor's and got my master's degree, and that was not all fun, but I liked school a lot more the second time around and my intuition said it was the right thing to do. I became an intern, then a clinical director, then I opened the Missing Peace and now I'm writing a book. All of this is from a whimsical trip to Sedona. Who knew that at the age of fifty-two, I would, at last, feel my true purpose? It is never too late to become who you were meant to be. It's not so much . . . *I came. I saw. I conquered.* It's more like . . . *I thought about going. I went. I turned around. I jumped to the left. I ran around in a circle. And then I came. I think. So I keep going.*

I was just, yes, I was following my bliss. To me, that's what the next right-indicated step means. What is the next move for me, that makes me happy and fulfills my purpose right now? I'm not talking about a quick fix that feels good for a second that I know ends badly. I'm referring to an opportunity that sounds fun and has meaning. I hope I continue to do this for the rest of my life.

Who knows what I will be at sixty-two or even seventy-two? I will keep following the path that makes me happy and I'll find out. The point is, the puzzle pieces of your life are creating a bigger picture that you can't see in the moment. Everything I have done from childhood until now were small parts of a whole in the making. A conscious effort to enjoy each piece will create a picture that brings you contentment, fulfillment, and purpose.

As you re-create your life, how you spend your days is most certainly a topic to consider altering if it is not bringing you joy. To experience self-actualization, as mentioned in chapter 10, you do not need to know what your future self or career is at this time. You only need to connect with the feelings you want to experience regularly. In chapter 10 you created a vision board. In chapter 29 you practiced sending thoughts and feelings for your desires into the quantum field.

It is time to get more specific. Let's focus on your passion and your driving force. Let's send the universe the frequency of your desired emotional state, and then remain open to opportunities that, "out of nowhere" seem to come your way. This is how it works.

## Build Your Toolkit

Get your My Re-Creation Manual. Take a look at the driving forces listed earlier.

1. Write down the category that fits you best.
2. Write down some words that you associate with that category—that is, freedom, notoriety, financial abundance, joy, accomplishment, peace.
3. Write down the kind of environment you want to be in indoor/outdoor, corporate, contractor, or at home.
4. Write down the number of hours you'd like to work.
5. Write down the things you need or would like time for besides work.
6. Now I want you to make a short video of yourself. You will speak into the camera as if all the things you wrote down have already happened. Use "I am" statements and say the words with gusto and confidence. Create the energy you want to connect with in the quantum field. It is out there already.

    For example:

    Hello Universe, I am Laura and I am grateful for my beautiful life. I am working outdoors. I am able to help people. I am free, I am making a difference. I am not a nine-to-five person. I am a person with a flexible schedule. I am making friends. I am stress-free! I am healthy. I am taking care of my family. I am respected. I am making my dreams come true.

7. Play this video for yourself every day for thirty days and keep yourself open to unexpected opportunities.
8. Feel free to make new a one after thirty days.
9. Here is the important part to remember. You are just taking the next right-indicated step. You don't know the end game or where it may lead, only that you want to enjoy the process.

# CHAPTER THIRTY-FOUR

~

# The Ups and Downs

On many days, I am raring to go. On some days I am not. Today was one of those days. The sun was shining, and nature was brimming with spring. I, on the other hand, was nestled on my couch under a blanket. I was not motivated to do anything other than watching black-and-white movies, and slowly make my way through a crossword puzzle or two. Despite my low mood, I felt comfortable and lucky to be in my pajamas at 3 p.m. on a Tuesday.

"You okay, Sweetie?" my husband asked as he passed from his office to the kitchen.

"Yep," I said. "Just havin' a pajama day."

My sister and I had written a song about pajama days. To the world, this may have looked like deep depression, but I knew differently. I knew I needed days to do nothing and feel my melancholy. Most people would peg me as an extrovert, but those who know me well understand that I am also an introvert. I had a patient who said it best. He called himself an ambivert. I think that describes most of us better than the extremes do. Sometimes I'm up and sometimes I'm down, and none of it is a bad thing.

I consumed a bowl of popcorn without noticing a bite of it. I got up for the occasional cup of tea. I dozed in and out and kept rewinding the movie to the parts where I drifted off. The phone rang, and I let it go to voicemail most of the time. Unless it was the office. Then I would address the issue and gladly return to my blah.

My Inner Critic and Wounded Child would chime in now and then, questioning if I'd ever have the energy or desire to go back to work, or if would I take the time to shower today. My Capable Adult Self reminded me that I would feel joy at the office tomorrow, and the state of my hair was rather unimportant at the moment. Sitting on the couch and doing nothing felt good. I was not do-ing. I was be-ing.

I stayed on the couch all day and evening. I went to bed early. The next morning found myself slow to get ready for work. *Another day on the couch would be great. You'll feel good at the office too.* I knew it was true.

I pulled into the driveway at work. I was still feeling pretty mellow. As I walked through the door, I saw a patient in the lobby.

"Good morning!" I smiled. My endorphins started kicking in.

"Hi," she said with low energy.

"How are doing today?" I put my hand on her shoulder.

"I feel pretty off," she mumbled.

"Take it easy today. Just do what you can. We can only do what we can do," I told her.

"Thanks, that takes the pressure off a little. I almost didn't come today." She gave a small smile.

"I totally get that," I reassured her as I went inside.

My energy had changed. I felt good. I was where I was supposed to be and glad to be there.

"Hey, Mama," I called out to my director of admissions, work-wife, and best friend.

"Hey lady. I've got some stuff for you to sign." She held up some papers.

I went into her office, and she caught me up on issues of the day. We laughed about her son's ongoing journey into puberty and the de-lusional remarks most recently made to me by my mother. It was going to be a good day.

## My Re-Creation Manual: Ride the Waves

No one can feel great 100 percent of the time. We all have ups and downs. To expect anything else would only be disappointing. Everything in this universe comes in waves. Light, sound, water, your pulse, and also your moods, come in waves. Ride the waves. Enjoy the ups and make space for the downs. It's normal and healthy.

It took me a long time to become a good wave rider. Calling myself a surfer creates too many funny visuals, so I'm going to stick with wave rider. I used to fear the downs. I worried that I had lost my drive or that I would steer off my intended course. Perhaps I associated lying around and doing nothing with the time I hit my bottom, and therefore it seemed wrong. But I think it's more along the lines that melancholy doesn't feel good. I am addicted to joy. I want to feel it all the time, but that's not natural or even possible. There is comfort to be found in the downs too.

My down times aren't depression, they are just days in which my body needs time to catch up with my brain. The part of my brain that says "go" is not in touch with my body, and left to its own devices, it will wear me ragged. Truth be told, moderation isn't my specialty. By nature, I am a doer. I have learned how to "be." I am getting better and better at recognizing my need for rest and have worked time into my schedule to do nothing. Sometimes it feels good and sometimes I feel drained. But no matter what, I know I am going to feel up again. I have learned about the waves, and I accept them.

I ride the waves with more interest now. Sometimes my downs are more introspective and coax me to identify what is causing me unnecessary drain or strife. Sometimes they're not. They are simply a break for my brain and my body.

To re-create the life you want, you must learn to recognize your waves, and not fight them. You must learn to ride them and find the gifts in the downs as much as the ups. Embrace all of you. Not just the parts that feel good. Fighting the waves creates anxiety as if something is supposed to be different. Riding the waves brings you peace and insight.

I have shared much with you throughout this book about how your anxiety works, how to harness it, and how to have better relationships with yourself, other people, and the universe. I want you to chase your dreams and achieve them because I know you can. But above all, I want you to love yourself. All of you. No matter what. The ups will drive you and the downs will guide you. Let your brain, body, and spirit become partners. Embrace them all. You'll have the ride of your life.

## Build Your Toolkit

1. Write yourself a love letter acknowledging all that you've done and all that you want to become.
2. Mail it to yourself.
3. Write today's date on the envelope and open it one year from the date you wrote it. See what transpired. I'll bet you're pleasantly surprised.

# Index

~

# About the Author

Laura Rhodes-Levin, LMFT, is a licensed therapist specializing in treating anxiety, depression, and trauma. She holds a master of science in counseling and is known for her original and successful approach to understanding anxiety and anxiety disorders. Five years ago, she founded The Missing Peace Center for Anxiety, a facility that offers a variety of modalities combining modern and ancient practices for mental disorders. Laura has appeared on several news shows, radio shows, podcasts, and magazines as a regular expert. She helped to create the Special Interest Group of Integrative Health for the Anxiety and Depression Association of America (ADAA), serving first as a co-chair and then as the lead chair. Laura has acted as the executive clinical director at Awakenings Treatment Center and as the director of meditation and neurofeedback at Promises Treatment Center in Malibu, California. She has led meditation groups every year for the past 12 years at the Sunlight of the Spirit Serra Retreat in Malibu. Laura is a fellow anxiety sufferer who has finally, at long last, through trials and tribulations, become friends with her brain. She is also a trained motivational speaker and ad-lib performer. She has appeared or been featured in *Good Day L.A*, *KTLA*, *KCBS*, *KCAL 9*, *KABC*, *CBS*, *Dr. Drew*, *Fox News*, *NBC*, *PBS*, *National News in Arizona*, *San Diego*,

*New Hampshire*, top-rated news and magazine articles from *Huffington Post*, *Bustle*, *Very Well Minded*, *Thrive Global*, *Women's World*, *Voyage L.A.*, *Formidable Woman*, *Be Kind & Co.*, *Medium*, *Highya.com*, *Valley News Group*, *The Local Optimist*, *Parade Magazine*, *Psych Central*, *The Zoe Report*, *USA Today*.